Dr Stephanie Coker is a barrister at FOURTEEN, a leading Family Law Chambers in London. She has a private family practice dealing with financial remedies following the breakdown of a marriage, as well as unmarried couples. She also advises on complex domestic and international private children matters and civil remedies following domestic abuse. Prior to coming to the Bar, she worked at leading law firms in which she gained a wealth of experience in contentious and non-contentious property matters. Outside of practice, she writes case summaries for the Financial Remedies Journal where she is an Assistant Case Editor. She has also taught Family Law, Property Law and Foundations of Property to undergraduates as well as Civil Advocacy and Opinion Writing to students studying the Bar Vocational Course.

A Practical Guide to Intervenors and Third Party Interests in Financial Remedy Proceedings

A Practical Guide to Intervenors and Third Party Interests in Financial Remedy Proceedings

Dr Stephanie Coker

Barrister, FOURTEEN

LLB (Hons), LLM, DPhil

Law Brief Publishing

Published 2025 by Law Brief Publishing, an imprint of Law Brief Publishing Ltd
30 The Parks
Minehead
Somerset
TA24 8BT

www.lawbriefpublishing.com

Paperback: 978-1-914608-97-1

To God my Heavenly Father without whom this book would not have been completed, and to my darling daughter Laelle who brings me smiles everyday

FOREWORD

A particularly knotty area of practice in the field of financial remedies is when third parties become involved. This may be the bank of mum and dad, poor old granny in her annex or a commercial entity of some appellation or other.

The treatment of "Intervenor disputes" in financial remedies are often poorly conceived, mis-managed and quickly take on a life of their own. Intervenor claims often end up becoming disproportionate in terms of costs and nearly always inflame bad feelings already reeling from the fact of a divorce.

The family practitioner needs to conduct an "intervenor dispute" differently to a standard *inter partes* financial remedy claim. There is much more emphasis on front loading and understanding the strengths and weakness from a black letter perspective. If the family lawyer engaged in a standard financial remedy dispute usually asks, "what would be a fair outcome?" those engaged in an "intervenor dispute" must first ask more alien and pedantic questions such as "who said what, where and when?" and "can I prove this?"

The family practitioner should beware of the unfamiliar terrain. An "intervenor dispute" is not a claim "for" a financial remedy and so the presumption against an order for costs does not apply. The "clean sheet" costs are a modified form of the Civil Procedure Rules (CPR) costs rules cut and pasted into the FPR. With the changes to the CPR from 1 October 2024, there is now an enhanced costs peril for those who enter into these waters without first trying NCDR/ADR first (CPR r.44.2(5)(e)). That rule should be carefully reflected upon. My personal experience is that many of these cases are best discussed in a civil/hybrid style mediation or debated in an Early Neutral Evaluation.

Dr Stephanie Coker has brought together in one handy volume the key authorities and statutory provisions that the busy family practitioner will need to have in mind in this tricky area.

I wish Stephanie well with this publication. Anyone who has been foolish enough to get talked into writing a legal textbook will know it is a huge endeavour and one which is not for the faint hearted.

Rhys Taylor
Barrister, The 36 Group
April 2025

CONTENTS

CHAPTER ONE

THE JURISDICTION OF THE FAMILY COURT AND THIRD PARTY INTERESTS

It is an established fact that any dispute between a spouse and a third party regarding the beneficial ownership of property can be adjudicated in financial remedy proceedings. As stated by Lord Denning MR in *Tebbutt v Haynes* [1981] 2 All ER 328:

> [242] It seems to me that, under s.24 of the 1973 Act, if an intervenor comes in making a claim for the property, then it is within the jurisdiction of the judge to decide on the validity of the intervenor's claim. The judge ought to decide what are the rights and interests of all the parties, not only of the intervenor, but of the husband and wife respectively in the property. He can only make an order for the transfer, to the wife, of property which is the husband's property. He cannot make an order for the transfer to the wife of someone else's interest. So, in order to make an order under s24, it must be within the jurisdiction of the judge to determine what are the various rights and interests in the property not only of husband and wife but also of any other persons who claim an interest.

Another intervenor case is *P v Q, R and S (Claim against Assets of Extended Family)* [2024] EWFC 164. In those proceedings, the court was concerned with a claim by the wife against the husband's parents who were joined as intervenors to the proceedings. The judge noted that it was not particularly clear what the wife's case was and stated that "it was not particularly clear during the hearing what the applicant's case is". This highlights the importance of complying with the guidance provided in paragraph 36 of *TL v ML*. Ultimately, the wife claimed to have a beneficial interest in some properties. The husband and intervenors argued that the facts do not support the case which the wife was advancing, and neither the wife nor the husband have any beneficial interest in either property.

The Family Court does not have the jurisdiction under the Trusts of Land and Appointment of Trustees Act 1996 ('TLATA'). It follows that TLATA claims must be issued in either a county court or the High Court, and not the family court. If a TLATA claim is to be heard together with an application under the Matrimonial Causes Act 1973 ('MCA 1973') or Schedule 1 of the Children Act 1989 ('Sch 1 CA 1989'), both claims will need to be heard at a combined county court and Family Court Centre or in the High Court. Notwithstanding this, it does not follow that the determination of what is or what is not 'property/financial resources' in financial remedy proceedings under the MCA 1973 is outside the jurisdiction of the Family Court. Indeed, it can be firmly stated that it is within the Family Court's dispositive powers under the MCA 1973 to make such determinations given the express reference to 'property/financial resources' under the section 25 statutory checklist.

In determining what property and/or financial resources are available for distribution, the Family Court applies trust law principles or proprietary estoppel principles which are universally applicable when determining property rights. According to section 31E(1) of the Matrimonial and Family Proceedings Act 1984 ('MFPA 1984') "*in any proceedings in the family court, the court may make any order (a) which could be made by the High Court if the proceedings were in the High Court, or (b) which could be made by the county court if the proceedings were in the county court*". Such orders include the power to make a declaration. On this basis, the family court has the power to make a declaration as to the beneficial interests without the jurisdictional issues that can arise as the family court is not exercising TLATA jurisdiction. In financial remedy proceedings between spouses, the court is required to perform an essentially inquisitorial role and then discretionary exercise pursuant to sections 23-26 of MCA 1973. In contrast, when determining the issue between a spouse and a third party as to who owns what, "the court is not performing a discretionary exercise but is determining issues of property law and associated fact".[1]

Having determined the beneficial ownership of a property, the declaratory relief will be binding against the whole world, and not just the parties and the intervenors to the claim. Support for this proposition is drawn the case of *Tebutt v Haynes & Anor* [1981] 2 All ER 238 which concerned a claim for a transfer of property between husband and wife under section 24 of MCA 1973. Mrs Tebutt claimed that she had a considerable interest in the house, and she was rightly brought in as an intervenor. Per Lord Denning MR:

> [242] It seems to that, under s24 of the 1973 Act, if an intervenor comes in making a claim for property, then it is within the jurisdiction of the judge to decide on the validity of the intervenor's claim. The judge ought to decide what are the rights and interests of all the parties, not only of the intervenor, but of the husband and wife respectively in the property. He can only make an order for the transfer, to the wife, of property which is the husband's property. He cannot make an order for the transfer to the wife of someone else's interest. So, in order to make an order under s24, it must be within the jurisdiction of the judge to determine what are the various rights and interests in the property not only of

1 *Goldstone v Goldstone & Ors* [2011] EWCA Civ 39, [2011]

> husband and wife but also of any other persons who claim an interest.

Although Bingham LJ refers to the Family Division, in light of section 31E MPFA 1984 it is clear that the same logic equally applies to the Family Court which also undertakes the same exercise in section 24 and may make similar orders as the High Court. In these types of cases, the task of the judge in determining ownership between a spouse and a third party is different from the discretionary exercise undertaken by the judge when determining issues between spouses. In *TL v ML & Ors (Ancillary Relief: Claim Against Assets of Extended Family)* [2005] EWHC 2860 (Fam), [2006] 1 FLR 1263, Mostyn QC (sitting as a Deputy High Court judge) stated that "a dispute with a third party must be approached on exactly the same legal basis as if it were being determined in the Chancery division".

In *Goldstone v Goldstone & Ors* [2011] EWCA Civ 39, the principal point in dispute was whether an issue between one of the parties to matrimonial finance proceedings and a third party as to the beneficial ownership of an asset subject to claim for a property adjustment order within the matrimonial proceedings should be determined as a preliminary issue within those proceedings or in a separate civil claim. In that case, Thorpe LJ emphasised that whilst the Family Court are exercising a fact-finding/declaratory jurisdiction in intervenor cases, and the substantive law may be property law, the procedural rules to be used are the Family Procedure Rules and not the Civil Procedure Rules. He stated that:

> [39] Of course, the ultimate trial required the family division judge to apply the law of property and the law of sham just as his brother judge would do in the Chancery Division. Careful preparation for that trial was necessary. However, these impeccable directions do not require or permit the import of the CPR. In its essence the claim remains a claim by the wife

> against the husband. Ultimately it is a claim for discretionary relief. In this, as in my cases, there must be a preliminary issue trial to establish the extent of the assets over which the discretion is ultimately exercised. Here, as in many cases, the preliminary issue trial determines the claims and the rights of third parties. The preliminary issue trial is pendent on the originating application. It has no independent existence.

The position is more procedurally complex if the third party commences their intervention by way of a free-standing TLATA claim in a county court by issuing either a Part 7 or Part 8 claim. Given that such is a civil claim, it would not be possible for the application or claim to be transferred to a family court such as the Central Family Court or the Financial Remedies Court ('FRC') so that the claim can be heard alongside proceedings under the MCA 1973. This is simply due to the lack of jurisdiction. If this occurs, an application should be made to the county court to stay those proceedings pending the determination of the beneficial interests in the family court or FRC. The TLATA proceedings in the county court can then either be dismissed on the grounds of res judicata or issue estoppel or restored for the purpose of enforcement by way of an order for sale. Directions can be made in the family court for the pleadings and any evidence in the county court claim to stand in the family proceedings. If the parties refuse to stay the civil proceedings, then a Hemain injunction restraining the relevant party from continuing with their actions should be sought and could be granted.

Given that financial remedy proceedings can involve and effect third parties, it is helpful to understand who are third parties? A third party is essentially an individual, body or entity that is not a main party to the proceedings. Within family law, there can be third parties in public and private child law proceedings as well as financial remedy proceedings. This book shall focus solely on financial remedy proceedings. In financial remedy matters, third parties can include trustees, beneficiaries, individuals such as family members, companies or commercial partners. This book will focus on the first two in separate chapters, with discussions as to the relevant law to be applied, practical and procedural guidance on joinder including service. Although companies are not considered in this book, the procedural rules and test for joinder are equally applicable and therefore users of this book can apply them accordingly.

Given the potential for third party interests to arise, the Family Procedure Rules 2010 ('FPR 2010') now contain a provision for third parties to be joined, known as 'joinder', into the proceedings. A financial remedy order will only bind those parties to the proceedings. It is therefore necessary to consider at an early stage whether to join a third party to the proceedings to ensure the determination made by the court is binding on them. However, with the involvement of a third party comes complexity, delay and the potential for massively increased costs, to the extent that, without careful case management, the expense of disposing of a preliminary intervenor claim can exceed the costs of the main financial remedy claim.

CHAPTER TWO

INDIVIDUALS AS THIRD PARTIES

This chapter focuses on individuals as third parties in financial remedy proceedings. In the financial remedy context, there are two main areas that an intervenor claim arises concerning individuals. These are property claims and loans, also known as the 'bank of mum and dad'. The former can manifest in two different scenarios. The first is where it is alleged that a party to the marriage is beneficially entitled to property held in the name of a third party, such as a relative. This can include a parent who could not obtain a mortgage, and/or where a family member has advanced capital towards the purchase of the property. The second is where it is alleged that property legally held by a party to the marriage is actually owned by a third party. These individuals who join the proceedings are typically known as 'intervenors', and their claims 'intervenor claims'. An intervenor claim effectively interposes a civil claim into a financial remedy application, with directions for statements of case, witness statements, and in some instances, there can be a preliminary issue hearing (*TL v ML* [2006] 1 FLR 1263).

In respect of loans, an issue to be determined could be the capacity in which the funds were advanced – i.e., as a loan, investment or gift. Determining these issues are very important in financial remedy proceedings as it is fundamental that the court understands what is available for distribution and to exercise its discretion over it. As noted by Hughes LJ in *Gourisaria v Gourisaria* [2010] EWCA Civ 1019 at [12], "the size of the cake should be ascertained before the knife is applied to it". The chapter begins by discussing the types of intervenor property claims and the applicable legal principles, and loans.

2.1. Property Claims

Most times, the first place for a prospective intervenor claim to arise is following the exchange of the parties Forms E where parties are required to list all the properties that they have a legal or beneficial interest, and to state the extent of such interest. This is currently required under section 2 of the Form E. It is important that parties provide full and frank disclosure in this respect to avoid allegations of non-disclosure. Also, if it arises that a main party to the proceedings does have a legal or beneficial interest in a property and this is not disclosed, it broods distrust between the parties. As a consequent, the party who has come to discover this new asset may decide to pursue matters further due to a lack of trust in the hope or belief that there are other assets a party is hiding. The result of this tends to be the parties incurring unnecessary legal fees. An example of this is *EC v JC* [2024] EWFC 175 (B), a financial remedies final hearing heard by DJ Hatvany. The assets were modest, and an unfortunate feature of the case was that both parties had incurred large costs, which made clearing the debt on both sides and enabling the parties to rehouse in properties they needed problematic. Whilst the case did not concern intervenors, the comments by DJ Hatvany demonstrate the consequence of failing to complete Forms E accurately:

> [42] At first blush, it seemed to me that the wife spent a great deal of money asking questions about historical assets with no value.
>
> [43] However, the husband did not help by providing wholly inaccurate information in his form E. This is a key document supported by a statement of truth. In that document the husband gives the value of X Ltd as £16,625 and the value of the London flat as £-630. When he was cross-examined about this, he was simply unable to provide any explanation.

> [44] This meant that the wife could no longer take anything the husband said at face value…
>
> [45] When the husband undervalued his business, this set into train an atmosphere of utter distrust between the parties and I now have a better understanding as to why the costs are as high as they are.
>
> [46] This made it very difficult for the wife's solicitors to take seriously the husband's various offers of non-court dispute resolution in circumstances where inaccurate information had been given.

The critical point in every intervenor claim involving property is that the law

> [66] "… differs importantly from the law to be applied between the wife… [as to the former] the court is not performing a discretionary exercise but is determining issues of property law and associated fact. It is salutary for family practitioners to keep the distinction clearly in mind".[2]

Given the high stakes in intervenor claims, it is very important that parties get the law right. An example of a hopeless intervention claim, and its resultant consequences in costs is *Uddin v Uddin & Ors* [2022] EWFC 75. This came before HHJ Wildblood QC who described the case as "a disgraceful example of how financial remedy proceedings should not be conducted".[3] The matter concerned a dispute between a married couple which, according to the trial judge, "should have been simple", but the wife made 'hopeless' claims that the husband held beneficial interests in two other properties and controlling

---

2 *Goldstone v Goldstone* [2011] 1 FLR 1926, per Hughes LJ at [66].

3 At para [200].

influence in a restaurant.[4] The total matrimonial pot was c.£730,000, but £200,000 were spent on legal fees.[5] Most importantly, HHJ Wildblood QC stated that "it is the costs, a significant proportion of which have been driven by the wife's dogmatic pursuit of the speculative and unprincipled trust claims and by the husband's dishonest portrayal of his position within the business".[6] In his judgment, HHJ Wildblood QC described the claim as "*feral, unprincipled and unnecessarily expensive financial remedy proceedings*".[7] Intervention proceedings can be catastrophically expensive. Now that courts are more than willing to make costs orders that result in one party receiving less than what is required to meet their assessed needs[8], it is important that parties proceed with caution and not embark on claims that are speculative and not forensically defensible.[9]

---

4 At para [7].

5 At para [10]

6 At para [11].

7 At para [1].

8 *VV v VV (No 2)* [2023] 1 FLR 194 for an example although the wife's financial remedy award remained very high, and her costs liability low given the egregiousness of her litigation conduct.

9 Examples of this point can be found at para [146] which states, "Regrettably, I think that it is extremely disappointing that the points that were made so clearly by the Respondent parties at the hearing in April about the applicable trust principles were not absorbed more carefully on behalf of the wife.... The very short passage, cited as coming from Jones v Kernott (which it does not), is not a complete analysis of the law. No further arguments about the applicable law were advanced on behalf of the claimant. I have no bundle of authorities. No mention was made by the wife's counsel of *Laskar v Laskar* [2008] EWCA Civ 347 or *Marr v Collie* [2017] UKPC 17. No explanation has ever been given as to why the wife

The applicable principles of an intervenor case are property and trusts law. These are discussed in further detail in the following chapter. Generally, financial remedy proceedings are largely forward looking with the court being concerned with achieving fairness in accordance with the principles under the Matrimonial Causes Act 1973 ("MCA 1973"). Unlike financial remedy proceedings, the law applicable in intervenor matters is generally backward looking and cares little with achieving fairness. Instead, intervenor claims often turn on who is to be believed about what was said and discerning the parties' intentions. Consequently, for family lawyers, when preparing statements or pleadings, these documents should focus more on what intentions can actually be established on the balance of probabilities. This is because these claims involve an argument over the parties' respective beneficial interests in the disputed property. From experience, these claims can be more troubling to litigate given the reliance on discussions often years old about each parties' respective interests.

2.2. Loans: 'The Bank of Mum and Dad'

In recent years, there has been an increase in parents financially assisting their adult children with property purchases by making capital advances. This has occurred for various reasons. Some include rising property prices and high interest rates, which make it difficult for first-time buyers to enter the property market without financial

---

asserts the beneficial interests that she does". See also para [152] "I have therefore examined the full range of trust principles that, conceivably, might apply and I have concluded that none of them assist the wife in her claims. In my opinion the wife's trust claims have been unprincipled and have stuck rigidly to the contentions made at the outset of these proceedings without there being any sufficient analysis of the evidence as it is has come in or the law applicable to it".

assistance. Also, informal arrangements between parents and their children are often without proper documentation, making it difficult to prove the actual nature of the financial contribution in future. Although this familial financial allowance allows their children to get on the property ladder, it is not without its risks. Indeed, it is increasingly common for family practitioners to find parents becoming embroiled in legal disputes following the breakdown of their child's relationship, where one spouse asserts that their parent is calling in money advanced as this was a loan. Frequently, what was once understood to be a generous gift, or informal loan can become a point of contention. In the absence of clear evidence to the contrary, the courts may interpret such advances as gifts.

How then should the court deal with these cases? Should the parents be joined as parties? The obvious advantage is that by joining parents as creditors, the court's decision will be binding on them. However, serious consideration should be given to whether joining the creditor is proportionate, in light of the quantum of the loan against the likely costs of joining a third party with statements of case on the issue.[10] Also, there are important differences between disputed loans and interests in property, with the latter being more compelling to join an alleged owner or co-owner of property. Some key differences include the fact that disputes over loans generally involve issues of fact and not law. For example, the questions for the court will be whether the money advanced, was a gift or a loan, and if a loan, was it a soft loan. By contrast, disputes over beneficial interests in land generally involve difficult issues of law as briefly highlighted above. Another key point to bear in mind is that money is interchangeable with other money and can be dealt with more proportionality with the other resources, whereas real property is not. Again, while the court has no power to order payment to a non-party (*Burton v Burton* [1986] 2 FLR 419,

---

10 Family Procedure Rules 2010, r 1.2.

Wodehouse v Wodehouse [2018] EWCA Civ 3009) a dispute over a loan might be resolvable by adjusting the capital division between the existing parties (spouses) upon one party's undertaking to pay the creditor.

In 2022, HHJ Hess gave important guidance on the treatment of family loans in financial remedies proceedings whilst delivering judgment in the case of *P v Q*.[11] This guidance is relevant to everyday practice as the issue frequently features in and out of court negotiations and during financial remedy litigation. According to HHJ Hess, the treatment of loans "raise some questions of law which are not uncommon in financial remedies cases". In this case, both parties' respective parents provided them with funds to enhance their lifestyles. In determining the issue of the family loans, the following guidance was offered:

> [19]
>
> (viii) The first question is whether the advances should be regarded (in strict legal terms) as gifts or loans. As a matter of general principle, for an advance of money to be a gift there must be evidence of an intention to give – the *animus donandi*...
>
> (ix) In the family court, however, that is not the end of the matter because the inclusion or exclusion of a technically enforceable debt in an asset schedule can depend on its softness/hardness. This is perhaps an elusive topic to nail down...

11 [2022] EWFC B9

Hess considered a number of authorities from which he distilled summary principles that should be applied in assisting determine whether the monies advanced are hard debt or soft debt:

(x) …

(a) Once a judge has decided that a contractually binding obligation by a party to the marriage towards a third party exists, the court may properly wish to go on to consider whether the obligation is in the category of a hard obligation or loan, in which case it should appear on the judges' computation table, or it is in the category of a soft obligation or loan, in which case the judge may decide as an exercise of discretion to leave it out of the computation table.

(b) There is not in the authorities any hard or fast test as to when an obligation or loan will fall into one category or another…

(c) A common feature of these cases is that the analysis targets whether or not it is likely in reality that the obligation will be enforced.

(d) Features which have fallen for consideration to take the case on one side of the line, or another include the following and I make it clear that this is not intended to be an exhaustive list.

The following factors have been identified as either on their own, or in combination, pointing toward an obligation being considered a hard debt or soft debt. They are as follows:

(e) Factors which on their own or in combination point the judge towards the conclusion that an obligation is in the category of a hard obligation include (1) the fact that it is an obligation to a finance company; (2) that the terms of the obligation have the feel of a normal commercial arrangement; (3) that the obligation arises out of a written agreement; (4) that there is a written demand for payment, a threat of litigation or actual litigation or actual or consequent intervention in the financial remedies proceedings; (5) that there has not been a delay in enforcing the obligation; and (6) that the amount of money is such that it would be less likely for a creditor to be likely to waive the obligation either wholly or partly.

(f) Factors which may on their own or in combination point the judge towards the conclusion that an obligation is in the category of soft include: (1) it is an obligation to a friend or family member with whom the debtor remains on good terms and who is unlikely to want the debtor to suffer hardship; (2) the obligation arose informally and the terms of the obligation do not have the feel of a normal commercial arrangement; (3) there has been no written demand for payment despite the due date having passed; (4) there has been a delay in enforcing the obligation; or (5) the amount of money is such that it would be more likely for the creditor to be likely to waive the obligation either wholly or partly, albeit that the amount of money involved is not necessarily decisive, and there are examples in the authorities of large amounts of money being treated as being soft obligations.

Having considered the factual circumstances of a specific case and the factors above, it is for the judge to determine whether money advanced are a hard obligation or soft one, and whether, if at all, the monies should be reflected in the ES2.

An example of the application of the guidance in *P v Q*, is *AXA v BYB* [2023] EWFC 251 (B) which was heard by Recorder Rhys Taylor. The husband had commercial debts of £70,000 and £32,787 of debts to a personal associate, which the judge assumed to be repayable.[12] The wife had £79,820 of debts she asserted were owed to family and friends, and £42,854 of debts to commercial entities. The court had evidence of a loan agreement between the wife and her parents, and another one with her brother. In regard to the monies advanced by her father and brother, the judge stated:

> [**129**] … Whilst there may be a bit of flex with the timing of repayments, I am satisfied that this is not largesse which either man can simply gift to W. They will need to money back at some point and the brother has borrowed on commercial terms in order to be able to advance this sum.
>
> [**130**] Applying the factors in P v Q, these can be viewed as softer than a commercial debt and in respect of the due date for repayment to family, do not reach end dates for a little while.

It was ultimately held that the wife's debts to her family were 'soft loans'. However, the loan to the wife's friend was also found to be 'a bit harder'. The judge noted at para 131 that "the money has been advanced due to friendship rather than a familial bond and the money is required back now. I find that W will feel rightly compelled to repay this sum as a matter of urgency". The judge heard evidence from the wife's father and brother, which the judge described as straightforward and helpful. No evidence was heard from the friend. It should be noted that neither of these third party individuals were joined to these proceedings, which highlights that in these types of claims, formal joinder may not be necessary. This is discussed further in Chapter 5.

12 At para 137.

CHAPTER THREE

PROPERTY CLAIMS: THE APPLICABLE LEGAL PRINCIPLES

3.1. Common Intention Constructive Trusts

3.1.1. Domestic consumer context

Express declarations of trust are determinative of beneficial ownership, unless the declaration can be set aside for fraud, mistake or undue influence (*Pankhania v Chandegra* [2012] EWCA Civ 1438). A declaration of trust is a legal document confirming the terms of which an asset, such as a property, is held on trust. The document usually records how much of the beneficial interest is owned by each party, as well as other terms that may be agreed between them. The legal owners generally hold the property on trust for themselves as beneficial owners. For example, if the legal ownership of the property is jointly held, it follows that both parties hold the beneficial ownership jointly. However, there are instances where individuals may hold the property on trust for someone else (such as the husband holding the beneficial ownership on trust for a family member) even if they do not benefit from the property. In such cases, a declaration of trust can be created separately to record that the whilst the property is owned solely by the husband, the beneficial interests belong solely to the family member. An express declaration of trust can also be completed by the parties ticking the box on the form TR1 to confirm the owners the portions of beneficial interest.

In the absence of an express declaration of trust, the court may find a beneficial interest arising from a resulting, implied or constructive trust. Since the House of Lords decisions in *Pettitt v Pettitt* [1970] AC

777 and *Gissing v Gissing* [1971] UKHL 3, it has long been recognised that common intention constructive trusts are trusts arising by operation of the law giving effect to the parties' otherwise unenforceable common intentions, when it would be unconscionable to allow one of them to resile from such intentions, typically when they have relied on such intentions to produce that outcome. The first question that the court will want to determine are the parties' intentions. In deciphering the parties' intentions, the court is essentially looking at the parties' words and actions and what they say about how they intended the property to be owned. The starting point is that equity follows the law. The law recognises that in certain situations, the beneficial interest in a property may not follow the legal title. In *Stack v Dowden* [2007] 1 FLR 1858, the House of Lords set out that:

> [68] The burden will therefore be on the person seeking to show that the parties did intend their beneficial interests to be different from their legal interests, and in what way. This is not a task to be lightly embarked upon. In family disputes, strong feelings are aroused when couples split up. These often lead the parties, honestly but mistakenly, to reinterpret the past in self-exculpatory or vengeful terms..."
>
> [69] In law, "context is everything" and the domestic context is very different from the commercial world. Each case will turn on its own facts. Many more factors than financial contributions may be relevant to divining the parties' true intentions. These include: any advice or discussions at the time of the transfer which cast light upon their intentions then; the reasons why the home was acquired in their joint names; the reasons why (if it be the case) the survivor was authorised to give a receipt for the capital moneys; the purpose for which the home was acquired; the nature of the parties' relationship; whether they had children for whom

they both had responsibility to provide a home; how the purchase was financed, both initially and subsequently; how the parties arranged their finances, whether separately or together or a bit of both; how they discharged the outgoings on the property and their other household expenses. When a couple are joint owners of the home and jointly liable for the mortgage, the inferences to be drawn from who pays for what may be very different from the inferences to be drawn when only one is owner of the home. The arithmetical calculation of how much was paid by each is also likely to be less important. It will be easier to draw the inference that they intended that each should contribute as much to the household as they reasonably could and that they would share the eventual benefit or burden equally. The parties' individual characters and personalities may also be a factor in deciding where their true intentions lay. In the cohabitation context, mercenary considerations may be more to the fore than they would be in marriage, but it should not be assumed that they always take pride of place over natural love and affection. At the end of the day, having taken all this into account, cases in which the joint legal owners are to be taken to have intended that their beneficial interests should be different from their legal interests will be very unusual."

[**70**] This is not, of course, an exhaustive list.

3.1.2. Non-domestic consumer context

Resulting trust principles are not generally deployed in the domestic consumer context, i.e. where the property was acquired as an *investment* as seen in *Laskar v Laskar* [2008] 2 FLR 589. The case of *Laskar* concerned a dispute over the beneficial interests held by a mother and daughter in a former council house where the family had previously lived for many years, and which they had purchased with a view to buy-to-let investment in their joint names under the statutory 'right to buy'. Unlike *Stack*, which concerned two parties in a long-term sexual relationship, who had purchased the property with the intention, and indeed occupied it, as their family home, in *Laskar* the property was purchased primarily as an investment. In upholding that constructive trust principles did not apply, Lord Neuberger stated:

> [17] ... In this case, the primary purpose of the purchase of the property was an investment not as a home. In other words, this was a purchase which, at least primarily, was not in "the domestic consumer context" but in a commercial context. To my mind it would not be right to apply the reasoning in Stack v Dowden to such a case as this, where the parties primarily purchased the property as an investment for rental income and capital appreciation, even where their relationship is a familial one.

Accordingly, Lord Neuberger applied the resulting trust principles, the result of which meant that the parties' respective shares would reflect the extent of their contributions to the purchase price, including the payment of mortgages.

However, the Privy Council in *Marr v Collie* [2017] UKPC 17 later suggested that whether the subject property is a family home, or assets purchased in a familial context as investments, the court was not obliged to adopt a resulting trust approach.[13] The facts can be briefly summarised. Mr Marr and Mr Collie were in a personal and intimate long-term relationship with each other. During their relationship, they acquired a number of properties and other items such as art, a boat and truck. There was no express declarations of trust. All properties, save for the couple's family home were purchased for the

13 [2017] UKPC 17

purpose of investment. This was a key issue in this case as it turned on whether in regard to the investment properties, a presumption of resulting trust should apply or whether the case should be treated as falling within the domestic consumer context, so that the resulting trust approach would not apply. The cash contributions of the purchase price relating to the investment properties was found to have been paid by Mr Marr, along with most, if not all, of the mortgage payments. Mr Collie's case was that it was the parties' intention that he would renovate the properties or that he would build on the plots of land acquired, and so, on that footing or in any case, all the properties were intended to be beneficially equally owned from the outset.

At first instance, the judge dealt with the family home applying the principles set out by Baroness Hale in *Stack*. In respect of the investment properties, the judge found that given that they were all purchased for non-domestic purposes, the resulting trust principles would apply and therefore Mr Marr was entitled to the entire beneficial interest in each. This decision was reversed before the Bahamas Court of Appeal which also applied *Laskar* but found that the presumption of resulting trust was rebutted by an email between Mr Marr and his solicitor indicating that he intended Mr Collie to hold beneficially 50% of the investment properties. Mr Marr appealed to the Privy Council. The appeal concerned the ownership of the properties and the other items and how they should be disposed of following the breakdown of their personal relationship.

In delivering the leading judgment, Lord Kerr reviewed the authorities and stated:

> [49] The Board does not consider, therefore, that *Laskar* is authority for the proposition that the principle in *Stack v Dowden* (that a conveyance into joint names indicates legal and beneficial joint tenancy unless the contrary is proved)

> applies only in "the domestic consumer context". Where a property is bought in the joint names of a cohabiting couple, even if that is as an investment, it does not follow inexorably that the "resulting trust solution" must provide the inevitable answer as to how its beneficial ownership is to be determined. Lord Neuberger did not intend to draw a strict line of demarcation between, on the one hand, the purchase of a family home and, on the other, the acquisition of a so-called investment property in whatever circumstances that took place. It is entirely conceivable that partners in a relationship would buy, as an investment, property which is conveyed into their joint names with the intention that the beneficial ownership should be shared equally between them, even though they contributed in different shares to the purchase. Where there is evidence to support such a conclusion, it would be both illogical and wrong to impose the resulting trust solution on the subsequent distribution of the property.

As seen above, Lord Kerr effectively concluded that there should be no difference in the correct approach in domestic and non-domestic cases, "save perhaps where there is evidence from which the parties' intentions can be identified".[14] The starting point in all situations, is the intentions of the parties. Lord Kerr concluded that context in this area of the law is everything and that, generally, the answer is not to be found by one presumption triumphing over another:

> [53] If what Lady Hale described as a "starting point" (that joint legal ownership should signify joint beneficial ownership) is to be regarded as a presumption, is it in conflict with the presumption of a resulting trust where the parties have contributed unequally to the purchase of property in their joint names? A simplistic answer to that question might

[14] See para [54].

be that, if the property is purchased in joint names by parties in a domestic relationship the presumption of joint beneficial ownership applies but if bought in a wholly non-domestic situation it does not. In the latter case, it might be said that the resulting trust presumption obtains.

[54] The Board considers that, save perhaps where there is no evidence from which the parties' intentions can be identified, the answer is not to be provided by the triumph of one presumption over another. In this, as in so many areas of law, context counts for, if not everything, a lot. Context here is set by the parties' common intention – or by the lack of it. If it is the unambiguous mutual wish of the parties, contributing in unequal shares to the purchase of property, that the joint beneficial ownership should reflect their joint legal ownership, then effect should be given to that wish. If, on the other hand, that is not their wish, or if they have not formed any intention as to beneficial ownership but had, for instance, accepted advice that the property be acquired in joint names, without considering or being aware of the possible consequences of that, the resulting trust solution may provide the answer.

3.2. Proprietary Estoppel

"One day, this will all be yours"

The document of proprietary estoppel is closely connected and broadly similar to those concept of common intention constructive trusts. This is because both doctrines are concerned with preventing unconscionable conduct and both doctrines are engaged, most commonly, where one party has made a representation to the other party concerning themselves acquiring an interest in or right over land, which the second party relied upon to their detriment. A notable difference is that proprietary estoppel is an equitable remedy which takes effect upon judgment of the court, whilst a common intention constructive trust is declared by the court to be the state of affairs existing at the relevant time. Given the overlap and similarity between both doctrines, the same set of facts may give rise to a remedy under either doctrine. However, there are important differences between both doctrines which should be noted.

The components of proprietary estoppel are set in *Thorner v Major* [2009] 1 WLR 776. When considering a proprietary estoppel claim the focus is on whether there has been an assurance of sufficient clarity from party A to party B, reasonable reliance on that assurance by party B and detriment to party B as a consequence of the reliance if party A resiles from its promise. Where this criterion is satisfied, an equity will be raised. Further useful principles were outlined by Lewison LJ in *Davies v Davies* [2016] EWCA Civ 463 at para 38. In this case, the judge provided a helpful summary of the principles derived from case law concerning establishing the equity for a proprietary claim:

> [38] Inevitably any case based on proprietary estoppel is fact sensitive; but before I come to a discussion of the facts, let me set out a few legal propositions:
>
> (i) Deciding whether an equity has been raised and, if so, how to satisfy it is a retrospective exercise looking backwards from the moment when the promise falls due to be performed and asking whether, in the circumstances which have actually happened, it would be unconscionable for a promise not to be kept either wholly or in part: *Thorner v Major* [2009] UKHL 18, [2009] 1 WLR 776 at [57] and [101].

(ii) The ingredients necessary to raise an equity are (a) an assurance of sufficient clarity (b) reliance by the claimant on that assurance and (c) detriment to the claimant in consequence of his reasonable reliance: *Thorner v Major* at [29].

(iii) However, no claim based on proprietary estoppel can be divided into watertight compartments. The quality of the relevant assurances may influence the issue of reliance; reliance and detriment are often intertwined, and whether there is a distinct need for a "mutual understanding" may depend on how the other elements are formulated and understood: *Gillett v Holt* [2001] Ch 210 at 225; *Henry v Henry* [2010] UKPC 3; [2010] 1 All ER 988 at [37].

(iv) Detriment need not consist of the expenditure of money or other quantifiable financial detriment, so long as it is something substantial. The requirement must be approached as part of a broad inquiry as to whether repudiation of an assurance is or is not unconscionable in all the circumstances: *Gillett v Holt* at 232; *Henry v Henry* at [38].

(v) There must be a sufficient causal link between the assurance relied on and the detriment asserted. The issue of detriment must be judged at the moment when the person who has given the assurance seeks to go back on it. The question is whether (and if so to what extent) it would be unjust or inequitable to allow the person who has given the assurance to go back on it. The essential test is that of unconscionability: *Gillett v Holt* at 232.

In simple terms, proprietary estoppel stops someone from going back on their promise. Proprietary estoppel allows the promisee to enforce a promise made by the promisor in relation to the ownership of lands where the promise has reasonably relied on that promise and suffer detriment if the promise was not fulfilled even though the promise is not supported by consideration as would be recognized in the law of contract.

What should be the remedy? The proper approach to granting relief under the doctrine of proprietary estoppel was considered in *Guest v Guest* [2022] UKSC 27. More specifically, the Supreme Court was asked to determine whether a successful claimant's expectations were an appropriate starting point when considering remedy, and whether the remedy granted went beyond what was necessary in the circumstances of that case. The majority, following the leading judgment of Lord Briggs, ruled that the primary remedy should be the enforcement of the promise. In essence, the claimant's expectations must be satisfied, while the minority, following the judgment of Lord Leggat, argued that the court's function was largely to compensate the claimant for their reliance (to their detriment) on the promise which would not be fulfilled.

While the test set out by Lord Briggs will be very helpful guidance going forward the question whether or not the fulfilment of the full promise is proportionate will be key. Furthermore, the court will be at pains to ensure a fair outcome for all parties involved and try to ensure that the defendant also does not suffer unnecessarily. Finally, when deciding the remedy, careful consideration needs to be taken when there is an acceleration of the promise. In those circumstances, both judgments agree, an appropriate discount in the award needs to be made.

CHAPTER FOUR

THIRD PARTY TRUSTEES AND TRUSTS ASSETS

An increasing number of people enter trust arrangements to save on inheritance tax and give flexibility to family arrangements for future generations. What then happens when a husband and wife set up a trust together and then decide to live apart? The court's approach to the trust assets in financial remedy litigation depends on the nature of a party's interest in the trust as well as the broader circumstances of the case. This chapter will also consider joinder of trustees and/or beneficiaries and the approach of the court to trusts within an application for a financial remedy in respect of it exercising its power to vary a nuptial settlement under section 24(1)(c) of the Matrimonial Causes Act 1973 ('MCA 1973'). The power to vary a trust which is an ante-nuptial or post-nuptial settlement is considerable, including even the power to exclude a beneficiary entirely from a settlement and to transfer an asset to a non-beneficiary free from the trust. This discussion is provided solely as a background to understanding how third party interests may arise in these cases.

4.1. Nuptial settlements

Section 24(1)(c) MCA 1973 gives the court the power to vary any ante-nuptial or post-nuptial settlement made on the parties to the marriage for the benefit of the parties to the marriage and the children of the family or either or any of them. It states:

> On making a divorce, nullity of marriage or judicial separation order or at any time after making such an order

> (whether, in the case of divorce or nullity of marriage order, before or after the order is made), the court may make any one or more of the following orders, that is to say –
>
> ...
>
> (c) an order varying for the benefit of the parties to the marriage and of the children of the family or either or any of them any ante-nuptial or post-nuptial settlement (including such a settlement made by will or codicil) made on the parties to the marriage, other than one in the form of a pension arrangement (within the meaning of section 25D below).

This provision is very significant as it effectively permits the court to access funds that are far greater than those disclosed as typical matrimonial assets. In theory, the power to vary a nuptial settlement is unlimited. However, the court will generally decline to interfere with a trust any further than is required in order to achieve fairness. The power of the court to vary a nuptial settlement is not limited to the interest held by the party before the court, but it extends to the entire trust. This point was made clear in *Brooks v Brooks* [1996] 1 AC 375, where Lord Nicholls stated at 392G-H:

> The section gives the court power to vary a settlement. Inherent in this provision is the notion that the court's jurisdiction extends to all the property compromised in the settlement. Thus, it includes any interest the settlor may have in the settled property by virtue of the settlement. Further, the court's power is not confined to varying the interests of the parties to the marriage under the settlement. The power includes, for instance, the interests in the settled property of the children or, more widely, of others under an old fashioned protective trust.

The power under section 24 can be exercised both where the interests of the beneficiaries are fixed, and also, importantly, where the allocation of settled property is at the discretion of trustees.[15] Therefore, as Lord Nicholls points out, property which in fact or in law might be regarded as available for the benefit of third parties can be made available to meet the claims of the applicant for financial relief arising from the breakdown of the marriage. Notwithstanding this, the court will be slow to deprive a third party of their legitimate expectations, and in most cases will do no more than divide a quart into two pints.

Furthermore, in *Ben Hashem v Ali Shayif* [2009] 1 FLR 115 Munby J set out five principles at paras 290 to 291. They are as follows: (1) Theoretically, the court's discretion is unlimited and unfettered. As mentioned above, its power can extend to excluding a beneficiary from the settlement or transferring assets to a non-beneficiary without the trust; (2) however, the court must begin with taking into account all factors under section 25(2) MCA 1973; (3) the aim is to achieve a fair outcome for both parties, looking at the matter as a whole; (4) the settlement should be interfered with as little as possible; and (5) in particular, the court should be slow to deprive innocent third parties of their rights, and if the court has to advance into new territory to achieve the settlement, the court should try and achieve an appropriate quid pro quo for the affected beneficiaries.

4.2. Should trustees be joined?

The relevant rules when considering joinder and the position of trustees are as follows: the overriding objective (FPR 2010 r 1), the requirement that a child be separately represented on an application to vary a nuptial settlement, save where the proposed variation does

15 *Vallance v Vallance* (1907) 77 LJP 33.

not adversely affect his rights (FPR 2010 r 9.11), requirement to serve trustees (FPR 2010 r 9.13) and adding and removing parties (FPR 2010, r 9.26(B)). Given the points highlighted in the previous section, the question of whether trustees should be involved or invited to intervene becomes a necessary one. The following are examples of when the question of joinder in respect of trustees and/or beneficiaries may arise. First, where there are any questions of varying a settlement, the trustees (even if offshore) should be served with the financial remedy application and *given the chance to intervene*. There is no requirement that trustees must be joined. This was shown in *DR v GR (Financial Remedy: Variation of Overseas Trust)* [2013] 2 FLR 1534. In this case, Mostyn J discharged as parties the trustees of a discretionary Jersey trust which the wife argued was a postnuptial settlement. Between paragraphs 19 and 37 of the judgment, Mostyn considered joinder of the trustees, an aspect of procedure which had bedevilled the case. The judgment also highlighted that generally there is no need to join trustees where a party seeks a variation of a nuptial settlement, although it may in some cases be desirable:

> [20] It would seem that there is an instinctive belief held by some practitioners that in a variation of settlement case the trustees must be joined and probably all underlying companies as well. As I will show, this is a belief which is built on foundations of sand.
>
> [21] From the very dawn of the judicial power to vary settlements the law has *not* required joinder of trustees. Instead, the rules require that notice of the application is given to the trustees and also to the settlor, if living [per FPR r. 9.13] …
>
> [22] It can be seen, therefore, that the default position in a variation of settlement case is that the *trustees should be served but should not be automatically joined.* Once served they can

file evidence in answer. They can then decide whether to participate only as witnesses or to seek to intervene (i.e. to be joined) and to be represented. It is up to them. But if they have been served in accordance with the rules, and do nothing, then it is clear beyond a shadow of a doubt that any variation order will be valid and binding on them. And, no doubt, countless valid variation orders have been made under the default procedure without joinder of the trustees.

...

[28] ... As I pointed out in *BJ v MJ (Financial Remedy: Overseas Trusts)* at paras [18]– [21] if trustees do not voluntarily participate at the very least as witnesses and give proper disclosure then they can hardly complain if robust findings are made about the realities of control and the likelihood of benefit. The inquiry will be done on the evidence before the court and the formal joinder of the trustees will not enlarge that evidence. It may be said that the obtaining of information for the inquiry might be better achieved if the trustees are parties but as against that there is the fact that if they are not parties orders for disclosure against them as nonparties can be obtained under FPR 2010 r 24.2 or, if the trustee is overseas, by means of the procedure in r 24.12 (in a non-EU case) or r 24.16 (in a EU case).

...

[31] It can be seen that the very limited extent to which enforcement of this court's order can be achieved in Jersey does not depend one jot on whether the trustees were joined to the proceedings, or even if they submitted to the jurisdiction. Further, if the assets are sited here then a successful applicant will likely seek to enforce a variation

directly here and will not involve the Jersey courts at all. And Jersey trustees will not be criticised by bowing to the inevitable and accepting a direct variation against UK assets ordered by this court.

[32] The requirements of r 9.26B(5) are important. The Part 18 procedure requires at least 7 days' notice to be given to the other party and the provision of evidence in support of the application is crucial. The period of notice would enable the other party to alert the trustees/companies so that they could either signify consent or appear at the hearing to oppose that application. The failure to give any notice or to provide any evidence deprived them of that obvious right. I asked Mr Southgate why the rule was disregarded, and he was unable to give me an answer. In the future I would expect the rule to be scrupulously complied with.

[33] The rules do, however, provide for one class of beneficiary to be mandatorily joined. Rule 9.11(1) provides:

> 'Where an application for a financial remedy includes an application for an order for a variation of settlement, the court must, unless it is satisfied that the proposed variation does not adversely affect the rights or interests of any child concerned, direct that the child be separately represented on the application.'

An example case in which the court concluded that the trustees should be joined is *Tchenguiz-Imerman v Imerman (Application for Joinder* [2014] 1 FLR 865. In this case, £130m was held in a trust structure, of which the beneficiaries were the husband's adult children from a previous relationship, the husband's parents, the parties' (minor) child and the husband's grandchild, but not either the husband or the wife. The wife applied to vary the trusts as nuptial settlements and applied to join the trustees. With the support of the adult beneficiaries, the trustees obtained orders from the Royal Court of Jersey and East Caribbean Supreme Court approving their non-participation in the proceedings. Later, the three adult children applied to be joined as parties to the proceedings in England. Despite expressing some reservations about the application, Moylan J concluded that it would be desirable to join the adult children. He stated:

> [31] … It will clearly assist with the investigation and resolution of the matters and issues raised in this case, as referred to above. Further, it would be consistent with the overriding objective. It will put the court in a better position to deal with the case justly. In my view it is also likely, in fact, to assist with enforcement.
>
> [32] It will assist with the investigation and resolution of the matters and issues raised in the case because, as parties, the adult beneficiaries will be subject to direct disclosure obligations deriving from their status as parties. They will be subject to cross-examination. They will be entitled to cross-examine other witnesses and the parties. All the factual and legal issues which they reasonably wish to raise can be ventilated and determined.
>
> [33] Joinder of all the named beneficiaries, save the husband's father and mother, in the circumstances of this case would be as close as it is possible to achieve to the direct participation of the trustees. These beneficiaries would all be bound by this court's decision. How, in those circumstances, I ask rhetorically, could the Royal Court of Jersey or the East Caribbean Supreme Court accept arguments to the effect that, having fully participated, the beneficiaries should be permitted to evade the consequences of any order that I might make?

> ...
>
> [40] There has been some debate during the course of the hearing as to what disclosure obligations will be imposed on the adult beneficiaries as a result of them becoming parties to these proceedings. In my view, as parties they would be under an obligation to disclose all documents relevant to the issues raised within these proceedings, which would include:
>
> (a) whether the trusts are or are not nuptial settlements;
>
> (b) what are the resources held within the trusts;
>
> (c) the manner in which the trustees would be likely to exercise their discretion; and
>
> (d) any other issue going to the likely ability to enforce any order which this court might make.

In *TM v AH* [2016] EWHC 572 (Fam) Moor J had to determine an application by the wife to vary a nuptial a settlement, and to join the trustees of two allegedly nuptial trusts as parties to the litigation. The court granted the wife's application and joined the trustees as parties to the litigation. In this judgment, his lordship disagreed with Mostyn J's conclusions in *DR v GR* that once the trustees had been served, matters could be determined without the need for them to necessarily be joined as parties. He commented:

> [10] I have to say that it is not my experience that the court regularly deals with such matters without joining the trustees. Indeed, my experience is to the contrary, namely that the trustees are joined when there is an application to vary the trusts of which they are the trustees. In *A v A and St George's*

> *Trustees*[16], a decision of Mr Justice Munby, now of course President of the Family Division, he made it very clear in argument, if not in his published judgment, that trustees had to be joined for orders to be binding upon them. I consider it a tenet of article 6 of the European Convention on Human Rights that requires a fair trial that trustees should be joined before a court varies the trusts of which they are trustees. It is hard to see how a court can make such an order without them being parties to that litigation, let alone to say that such a variation is binding on them in such circumstances.
>
> [11] I have therefore come to the extremely clear conclusion that there is an existing matter in dispute in this case which requires for its resolution the joinder of a new party, namely these trustees. I am not making any comment whatsoever on the effect that joinder may have in either the BVI or Switzerland. It seems to me that that is irrelevant. This wife is applying to make very substantial changes to these trusts. The trustees should be joined so that they can have their say, if they wish to do so, on those very serious applications.

Second, adding trustees as a party may be necessary where a spouse is a beneficiary to a trust and the assets held within the trust are said to constitute a 'resource' of that beneficiary that should be taken into account following the authorities resulting from *Thomas v Thomas* pursuant to section 25(2)(a) MCA1973. Third, where one spouse alleges that property held in the name of a third party such as a trustee is beneficially owned by the other spouse.

Fourth, joining the trustees as a party may be necessary in circumstances where one spouse alleges that a settlement of property made by one of the parties is a 'sham' and that the property has always

16 *A v A* [2007] EWHC 99 (Fam); [2007] 2 FLR 467

remained the property of the spouse, and they have never divested themselves of it. Fifth, where one spouse alleges that property held in the name of a third party such as a trustee is beneficially owned by the other spouse. Sixth, joining the trustees are necessary to enforce the court's order or where joinder of the trustees and/or beneficiaries will make enforcement easier. Finally, documents that are relevant to the issues in the proceedings are in the power of the trustees and/or beneficiaries. Examples include those documents that go to the question of whether a trust is a nuptial settlement capable of variation and/or to obtain disclosure of information. Some of these relevant documents include trust accounts showing the value of assets held within the trust structure; documents concerning the manner in which the trustees have exercised or are likely to exercise their discretion e.g. the settlor's letters of wishes, minutes of meetings held by the trustees, or a request by a beneficiary for a formal explanation of the trustees future intentions; and core trust document such as the original trust deed and any subsequent deeds of variation.

4.3. Adding trustees as a party

As will be discussed in the following chapter, the test for adding new parties such as trustees and/or beneficiaries is set out in FPR r 9.26B. The test remains one of desirability. In essence, the applicant for joinder must show either that it is desirable to add the new party so that the court can resolve all the matters in dispute in the proceedings, or there is an issue involving the new party and an existing party which is connected to the matters in dispute in the proceedings, and it is desirable to add the new party so that the court can resolve that issue. In the case of the former limb, the applicant must clearly show that the existing matter in dispute between the third party and the applicant cannot be effectively and validly resolved without the third party being joined. In respect of the second limb, it must be shown that it is desirable for the separate issue to be heard together with the main proceedings. The question of whether it is desirable to hear the matters together extends to the commonality of evidence, as well as the saving of costs. If a new party is added because it is believed that joinder will lead to better enforcement in a foreign jurisdiction, there must be evidence that the joinder will actually make a difference. It is not enough to merely assert statements of belief.

Trustees should be served with an application and given the opportunity to intervene within the proceedings where there is a question of varying a settlement.[17] In these circumstances, the trustees have the following options. The first is that trustees can apply to be joined as a party to the proceedings. This route exposes the trust fund to legal costs, but this may be a more sensible option as by joining the proceedings, trustees will be able to present the beneficiaries case and be bound by (and benefit from) any determination given by the court. The second option is to co-operate with the parties to the main suit by giving information and disclosure subject to their duty of confidentiality owed to other beneficiaries. The duty of confidentiality owed by trustees to beneficiaries means that a trustee cannot provide a non-beneficiary party or their lawyers with detailed disclosure of a trust, its assets or the affairs of the beneficiaries. When trustees are faced with requests for disclosure from non-beneficiary parties, they will usually decline to provide such information and instead, if appropriate, provide them to the beneficiaries, knowing that they will be disclosed to the other party.

The third and final option is that, unfortunately, trustees may decide may choose not to disclose documents and information, possibly because it may not be in the best interests of all beneficiaries. However, this option can be construed by the court as obstructive and put the beneficiaries at risk of being accused of non-disclosure, and the court may draw adverse inferences accordingly. These issues were discussed

17 Family Procedure Rules 2010, r 9.13.

in *BJ v MJ (Financial Remedy: Overseas Trusts)* where Mostyn J suggests that if non-cooperation is encountered, the claimant should give thought to serving adult beneficiaries in order to ascertain their views about the proposed rearrangement.[18] An example of this can be seen in *Imerman*, the trustees of various Jersey and BVI trusts declined to participate in the proceedings, whereas the adult beneficiaries (who had an interest in opposing the wife's attempt to classify the settlements as 'nuptial') successfully applied to be joined as parties.[19]

Serving an application on trustees is not the same as joining the trustees as parties to the proceedings and does not have effect.[20] The decision as to whether an application should be made to join trustees to proceedings will be case specific. An order to join trustees (or to discharge them) can be made by the court of its own initiative pursuant to FPR r 9.26B(4), on an application by an existing party or on an application by the proposed additional party such as the trustee. The rules for service of documents such as the financial application in Form A on trustees in this jurisdiction of England and Wales can be found in FPR r 6.23. Pursuant to these rules, the Form A may be served by personal service (in accordance with rule 6.25); first class post, document exchange or other service which provides for delivery on the next business day, in accordance with Practice Direction 6A; leaving it at a place specified in rule 6.26 or by fax or email in accordance with Practice Direction 6A. Rule 6.35 provides the court with the court to permit alternative modes of service or at an alternative place. Documents served in accordance with these rules is deemed served on the day shown in the table found in FPR rule 6.34.

---

18 [2012] EWHC 4277 (Fam).

19 *Tchenguiz-Imerman v Imerman (Application for Joinder)* [2012] EWHC 4277 (Fam).

20 *T v T and others (Joinder of Third Parties)* [1996] 2 FLR 357

The rules for service of the financial application on trustees outside of the jurisdiction of England and Wales can be found in FPR r 6.40 onwards together with Practice Direction 6B. Those rules also set out the procedure for service. The following two provisions should be noted. No permission of the court is required before any document is to be served out of the jurisdiction.[21] Service should be in accordance with the law of the country in which service is to be effected, and it may be made either: (i) by the applicant his agent (if this is allowed under the local law of the country in which they are to be served); or (ii) through the relevant foreign government judicial authority.

In summary, Mostyn J offered the following comprehensive guidance on joinder in *DR v GR (Financial Remedy: Variation of Overseas Trust)* [2013] 2 FLR 1534 which is as follows:

> [35] Drawing the threads together it seems to me that the applicable principles on the question of joinder are as follows:
>
> (i) Joinder either of trustees or of the underlying companies is *not* an essential pre-condition for the validity of a variation of settlement order.
>
> (ii) However, it is mandatory for beneficiaries under the age of 18 to be joined unless the court can say that the proposed variation does not adversely affect the rights or interests of any such child. The court has power to modify this requirement but should be very sparing in its exercise. Failure to comply with this rule will not nullify any order later made. The application to join minor beneficiaries should be

21 FPR 2010, r 6.41.

made at the first appointment following the issue of the application.

(iii) The applicant, respondent, and the trustees and/or companies themselves can apply for joinder, but in each instance both the substantive terms of, and the procedure prescribed in, FPR 2010 9.26B must be carefully complied with.

(iv) The applicant for joinder must show either:

(a) that there is an existing matter in dispute which requires for its resolution the joinder of the new party, or

(b) that there is a matter in dispute between a party and the proposed new party which is connected to the main matters in dispute between the parties and that it is desirable to resolve all the issues together.

(v) Under the first limb it must be clearly shown that an existing matter in dispute between the parties cannot be effectually and validly resolved without the joinder of the proposed new party.

(vi) Under the second limb it must be shown that there is a separate dispute between a party and the proposed new party and that it is desirable to hear the matters together. The question of whether it is desirable to hear the matters together extends to the commonality of evidence as well as the saving of costs.

(vii) If better enforcement of an order in a foreign jurisdiction is relied on under either limb there must be evidence that joinder would actually make a difference. Mere assertion or statements of belief will not suffice.

(viii) An application for joinder must be made on notice under the Part 18 procedure, which requires 7 days' notice. Although the application strictly speaking does not need to be served on the proposed new party it would be better in the future if it were. The application must be supported by clear evidence.

CHAPTER FIVE

JOINDER – PROCEDURE AND CASE MANAGEMENT IN FINANCIAL REMEDY PROCEEDINGS

5.1. Judicial Guidance on Procedure to Intervenor Claims

Most family law practitioners will be familiar with the guidance of Mostyn QC (sitting as a deputy high court judge) in *TL v ML and Others (Ancillary Relief: Claim Against Assets of Extended Family)* [2005] EWHC 2860 (Fam) regarding the procedure to be adopted in intervenor claims. In this case, the total assets amounted to about £560,000, and the total costs incurred by the wife, husband, and intervenors were £474,278. The reason the parties racked up so much money was due to the wife asserting that other assets, held either by the husband's brother, or in offshore companies, were beneficially the property of the husband. The wife's secondary position was that the assets belonging to the husband's father and mother amounted to 'resources' within the meaning given in *Thomas v Thomas* whereby the courts should 'judicially encourage' them to meet her claim.

A key feature of the case was that the issue of the third party interest had not been properly defined, pleaded or particularised, and at no stage since the First Appointment had this discrete issue been the subject of any case management, notwithstanding that the parties had been before the court on numerous occasions. In addressing the procedure, the court noted as follows:

> [34] It is to be emphasised, however, that the task of the judge determining a dispute as to ownership between a spouse and a third party is, of course, completely different in nature from

the familiar discretionary exercise between spouses. A dispute with a third party must be approached on exactly the same legal basis as if it were being determined in the Chancery Division

[35] Mr Brett [counsel for the intervenors] makes the valid complaint that this issue has never been properly defined, pleaded or particularised. At no stage since the first appointment has this discrete issue been the subject of any case management, notwithstanding that the parties have been before the court on numerous occasions.

[36] In my opinion, it is essential in every instance where a dispute arises about the ownership of property in ancillary relief proceedings between a spouse and a third party, that the following things should ordinarily happen:

(i) The third party should be joined to the proceedings at the earliest opportunity

(ii) Directions should be given for the issue to be fully pleaded by points of claim and points of defence;

(iii) Separate witness statements should be directed in relation to the dispute; and

(iv) The dispute should be directed to be heard separately as a preliminary issue before the financial dispute resolution (FDR).

[37] In this way the parties will know at an early stage whether or not the property in question falls within the dispositive powers of the court and a meaningful FDR can take place. It also means that the expensive attendance of the third party for the entire duration of the trial can be avoided. It is a great pity

> that none of these steps took place in this case. Had they happened, I believe that a great deal of costs would have been saved."

This guidance was considered by Munby J (as he then was) in *A v A* [2007] 2 FLR 467:

> [23] … I am sympathetic to the approach being suggested by the deputy judge, though I would not wish to be quite so prescriptive as he appears to be. Vigorous judicial case management in such cases is vital, but the appropriate directions to be given in any particular case must reflect the case managing judge's appraisal of how, given the forensic realities of the particular case, the issues can best be resolved in the most just, effective and expeditious manner.
>
> [24] I do, however, entirely share the deputy judge's view that directions should normally be given for such issues to be properly pleaded by points of claim and points of defence. In the present case the muddle, confusion and ambiguities in the wife's case would have been more pitilessly exposed, and at a much earlier stage in the proceedings, had the presentation of her case been exposed to the intellectual discipline which is one of the advantages of any system of pleading. Moreover, if the wife had been required to plead her case everyone would have had a much clearer idea, and at a much earlier stage, as to exactly what she was or was not asserting and as to exactly what the husband and the intervenors were or were not saying by way of defence. As it was, matters were wholly unclear even as late as the first day of the final hearing.

Munby LJ (as he then was) also made the case for pleadings in intervenor cases in *KSO v MJO, JMO and PSO* [2008] EWHC 3031 (Fam). He stated:

> [55] This is not, I emphasise, a call for formality for the sake of formality. It is not a call for a return to a system of the arid technicality which, at least in legal folklore, will always be associated with the name of Parke B. It is, on the contrary, a suggestion for the wider adoption of a sensible and appropriate practice that might do something to stop, in their tracks and before ruinous costs are incurred, cases which, even if not, as sometimes, devoid of all merit, are unlikely to be of any real profit to those tempted to pursue them...

In *Goldstone v Goldstone* [2011] EWCA Civ 39, the Court of Appeal endorsed the directions given by Mostyn in *TL v ML*. That case concerned the central question of whether the preliminary issue, which concerned the husband's ownership and control of assets held in the Jeeves group, was governed by the Family Procedure Rules 2010 ("FPR") or the Civil Procedure Rules ("CPR"). Per Thorpe LJ:

> [39] ... these impeccable directions do not require or permit the import of the CPR. In its essence the claim remains a claim by the wife against the husband. Ultimately it is a claim for discretionary relief. In this, as in many cases, there must be a preliminary issue trial to establish the extent of the assets over which the discretion is ultimately exercised. Here, as in many cases, the preliminary issue trial determines the claims and the rights of third parties. The preliminary issue trial is pendent on the originating application. It has no independent existence.

Having made clear that the FPR are the rules that govern the joinder of intervenors, the FPR were amended after the decision in *Goldstone* to give the court a wide discretion to add third parties to any financial remedy proceedings if it is desirable to do so and later remove them. The principle underlying the rules on joining a party was considered by Hughes LJ in *Goldstone v Goldstone* [2011] 1 FLR 1926 (albeit in reference to CPR r. 19.2, upon which FPR r. 9.26B is closely modelled):

> [57] The principle underlying these rules is very clearly that it is desirable to equip a single court with the means of deciding all relevant connected issues within the same proceedings and to avoid a multiplicity of different and potentially conflicting proceedings.

5.2. The 'Desirability' Test: The Family Procedure Rules

The relevant rules for *Adding or Removing Parties* can be found in FPR r. 9.26B. These rules apply regardless of whether the prospective intervenor is a trustee, an individual or a company. The following points are important to note from this provision:

(i) r 9.26B(1): The court may direct that a party or body be added as a party to the proceedings if:

> "(a) it is desirable to add the new party so that the court can resolve all the matters in dispute in the proceedings or
>
> (b) there is an issue involving the new party and an existing party which is connected to the matters in dispute… and it is desirable to add the new party…".

(ii) r 9.26B(2): On the other hand, the court may direct that any person or body be removed as a party if it is no longer desirable for that person or body to remain a party to the proceedings.

(iii) r 9.26B(3): Where the court directs that a person or body are to be added or removed under the rule, "a copy of the application form or other relevant documents" may be served on the new party, and consequential directions may be given in respect of the management of the proceedings.

(iv) r 9.26B(4): The addition or removal of a party may be exercised either on the court's own initiative or following an application by an existing party or person or body that wishes to become a party.

(v) r 9.26B(5): "An application for an order under this rule must be made in accordance with the Part 18 procedure and, unless the court directs otherwise, must be supported by evidence setting out the proposed new party's interest in or connection with the proceedings…"

The rules above show that the court must be persuaded that the addition of the new party is desirable. In assessing desirability, some of the advantages of having the party join the proceedings can assist in persuading the court that they should be joined. In the right case, these advantages include the new party assisting the court in the investigation and resolution of key issues between the parties. This is because once a third party is joined to the proceedings, they become subject to direct disclosure obligations which naturally derive from their party status. The third party may also be cross-examined. Desirability may be because by adding the third party, the determination of the court in respect of the disputed issue or property will bind the third party and become enforceable against them.

In *KSO v MJO, JMO and PSO* [2008] EWHC 3031 (Fam), it was argued that joinder was justified to "find out" if there was a claim against the father-in-law or to 'get the full picture'. Munby LJ stated:

> [48] … I do not accept this. It seems to me, with all respect to Mr Turner, to confuse a person's involvement as a potential

> witness or source of disclosure (discovery in old-fashioned terminology) with his involvement because there is, within the meaning of rule 6(2)(b)(ii), some "question or issue" existing between him and some other party to the proceedings. RSC Order 15 rule 6(2)(b) applies in the latter but not, as it seems to me, in the former case. And, I might add, Mr Turner's proposition goes beyond anything to be derived from *T v T and others (Joinder of Third Parties)* [1996] 2 FLR 357."

Furthermore, joinder should not be pursued to give a third party an opportunity or platform to put their views more forcefully. This was shown in *JB v MB* [2015] EWHC 1846 (Fam) where at an earlier hearing Mostyn J heard an application for a company to intervene within the proceedings pursuant to FPR r 9.26B(1)(a). Mostyn determined that:

> [48] …the rule was not intended for the purpose for which it is advocated by Mr Thorpe at all which is simply to put a third party on a better footing to advocate its point of view. That can be done by the husband here and by witness statements which have already been made by the other shareholders and directors of the company and so I regard this application as being completely misconceived and it is dismissed.

It is tempting to want to oppose an application to join a third party to the financial remedy proceedings due to the consequent reduction in equity that can arise by a successful third-party claim, which can lead to a demonstrable reduction in housing capital post-separation. As understandable as these concerns may be, the fact that a successful claim by a third party may not be helpful to a party's case is not a good reason to oppose jointing the third party. It is important for parties to be objective.

Once a party is joined to the proceedings, it does not follow that they should receive wholesale disclosure. This was demonstrated in *Bogolyubova v Bogolyubov & Joint Stock Company Commercial Bank "Privatbank"* [2022] EWFC 199. In that case, Peel J considered an application by the bank, inter alia, to intervene in financial remedy proceedings and for specific disclosure. The application to intervene was permitted as the test in r 9.26B(1)(b) was clearly met. However, the application for specific disclosure sought by the bank was refused as it was viewed as unnecessary. At para 43, Peel J stated that they would "not be entitled to disclosure of any documents within the financial remedy proceedings unless agreed by the parties or ordered by the court". It follows that disclosure of any further documents can only be permitted if agreed between the parties or ordered by the court.

The issue of requests for specific disclosure by intervenors was also considered in *LS v PS* [2021] EWHC 3508 (Fam). In this case, Roberts J considered an application by an intervenor, litigation funding entity, for disclosure of material and information that was currently subject to 'without prejudice' privilege. At the heart of the dispute, was an allegation by the intervenor that the settlement reached at a private FDR was deliberately structured in a way to leave the wife with no assets or entitlement to property or liquid capital from which she would repay her debts to the company. The intervenor already had access to some financial disclosure generated during the proceedings, which it planned to use, together with the privileged material sought, in support of their set aside application to prove their case. The application for disclosure of material and disclosure that was subject to without prejudice privilege was refused, citing competing policy considerations, and referring to the "absolute bar" on the use of anything said or done at a FDR in support of a separate action in civil proceedings. However, the judge was not minded to descend into wider issues of the scope of the circumstances in which a party can disclose to a third party without the consent for other documents generated during the court of litigation.[22]

Save for where an intervenor is joined at the court's own initiative under FPR 9.26(B)(4), the Part 18 procedure "must be" followed, although this generally is not the case. The procedure is as follows. An application notice must be filed at court, and FPR r. 18.7 provides that the application must state what order is being sought and the reasons for the order sought. A draft of the order sought should be attached to the application notice.[23] The application should be supported by evidence setting out the proposed new party's interest in or connection with the proceedings, or the reasons for the removal of a party, where this is sought.[24] The application notice should be made on notice to each of the respondents and served in accordance with the provisions in FPR 2010 r. 18.8 and at least 7 days' notice must be given of the application.[25]

As well as joining third parties to the financial remedy proceedings, r 9.26B above highlights the power of the court to remove third parties. This is in line with the duty of the court in furthering the overriding objective by actively managing cases. Specifically, see FPR r.14(2)(b)(ii) which states that active case management includes "identifying at an early stage who should be a party to the proceedings". In *NW v BH* [2024] EWFC 118 (B) the husband's mother intervened in the proceedings in relation to ownership of the family home. Taken at its highest, the husband's mother's pleadings did not assert a beneficial interest in a property, but rather an assertion that the husband or both the husband and wife owed her £185,000.

---

22 See para [91].

23 Family Procedure Rules 2010, r 18.7(2).

24 Family Procedure Rules 2010, r 9.26B(5).

25 Family Procedure Rules 2010, r. 18.8 (b)(i).

The unsatisfactory nature of the husband's and his mother's evidence and their accountant's evidence, together with a lack of sufficient supporting evidence meant that Recorder Taylor did not accept that the husband's mother was owed £185,000. If there were any loans, they were soft loans. Recorder Taylor found that her 'doomed intervention was ill conceived'. The husband's mother was subsequently removed as a party under FPR 9.26B(2).

5.3. Relevant Directions

Typically, the appropriate directions in these types of cases are as follows. There should be service of the Form A and relevant parts of the Form E on the intervenor.[26] Joining an intervenor to the proceedings does not necessarily mean that they should receive the parties' entire Forms E. Only those parts that concern the intervention should be shared with the intervenor. Directions should also be made for the parties to file and serve statements of case. For the intervenor, they should file points of claim. Points of claim are not the same as a witness statement and they should not contain exhibits. Unless directed otherwise, it is sufficient to identify the documents that the intervenor plans to rely upon but not wholescale copying and pasting unless they are short and directly relevant. The points of claim should only assert those facts and legal principles found to be relevant in the case for the purpose of formulating a complete cause of action. The particulars should address the circumstances of any discussions or arguments. They should be used to provide commentary upon the other party's claim.

Points of claim do not require that there should be references to case law. The points of claim may also give the name of any witness the intervenor proposes to call. The essence of providing points of claim

26 Family Procedure Rules 2010, r 9.26B(3).

at an early stage is that is exposes parties claims to intellectual discipline, which allows the spectrum of the dispute to be set. Failure to have points of claim or the intervenor case clearly set out, can create ambiguity. A case showing the importance of having points of claim is *Uddin v Uddin*. In *Uddin*, the *TL v ML* directions were clearly not followed. This non-compliance led to the parties incurring £200,000 in costs whilst the asset base was worth £730,000.

The main parties to the suit should then be directed to file and serve a defence or 'points of defence'. Alternatively, where one of the parties supports the intervenor, consideration should be given for the sequential filing of the defence, with the party who opposes the intervenor claim going last. The Civil Procedure Rules provides some guidance on what the defence should address. Pursuant to CPR 16.5, the defence must deal with every allegation in the points of claim stating which of the allegations are denied, those that are unable to admit or deny, but which the intervenor is required to prove and those allegations that they admit to. Where a party denies an allegation, they must set out their reasons for doing so, and if they intend to advance a different version of events from that put forward by the claimant/intervenor, they must state their own version. It is sometimes appropriate to allow for a reply. Once directions for pleadings have passed, this allows all parties to know what the other parties are asserting as matters of fact and law. Given the cases that the parties have pleaded, a case management decision will need to be made concerning the type of disclosure that should be provided.

Directions should be made for disclosure by list and inspection. As pointed out by Moylan J in *Tchenguiz-Imerman v Imerman* [2014] 1 FLR 232, the FPR do not provide for a disclosure regime for parties to family proceedings. Instead, parties must work on the common law principles as expressed in Part 31 of the CPR. There are two types of disclosure under the CPR. The first is standard disclosure which is covered under CPR 31.3. Standard disclosure involves a party setting out either in a list or questionnaire, the documents material to the proceedings of the existence of which that party is aware, and which are or have been in that party's control. This is followed by inspection. More commonly, courts may direct that the parties serve those documents upon which they intend to rely when sending their Points of Claim and/or Defence. If proper disclosure has not been made, then specific disclosure can be sought.[27]

In family proceedings, specific disclosure entails where a party must disclose documents or classes of documents specified in the order, carry out a search to the extent specified in the order, or disclose any documents located as a result of that search. It is not uncommon in family proceedings for disclosure and inspection to be merged, with the list acting as an informal index to documents which are being shared and those that are being shared at the same time. Equally, the principle of standard disclosure may be applied in a less formal manner without the requirement of a list, but instead the court directing that the parties serve questionnaires and request for documents. This approach still retains the requirement that each party signs a statement of truth that all relevant documents have been disclosed.

Once the pleadings and documents have been prepared, the parties will then be in a position to file witness statements. In doing this, parties should bear in mind the requirements of the *President's Memorandum: Witness Statements dated 10 November 2021*. The provisions of FPR 2010, PD 22A para 3.3, PD 27A para 5.2, paragraph 22 of the Efficiency Statement of 11 January 2022, and any case-specific case management directions also need to be adhered to. After statements have been exchanged (the parties having set out their case sequentially in their pleadings), the matter can be listed for a preliminary issue hearing or further directions hearing or FDR appointment, depending on what the court decides. If the dispute is

27 Family Procedure Rules 2010, PD21A 2.4.

heard before the FDR, it allows the parties to know what assets are available for distribution as well as the court.

Whilst *TL v ML* is the 'gold standard' to be followed in joinder cases, this case management approach can sometimes be disproportionate in costs. A similar view was expressed by Munby J (as he then was) in *A v A (St George Trustees Ltd, Intervenors)* [2007] EWHC 99 (Fam), and which Mostyn acknowledged in *Fisher Meredith v JH and PH (Financial Remedy: Appeal: Wasted Costs)* [2012] 2 FLR 536 at [41] stating, "it is fair to say that while this discipline is generally speaking, the right way of proceeding, it is by no means a mandatory prescription". As stated by HHJ Evans-Gordon *et. al*:

> "... Provision for pleading and then disclosure without the further cost of statements being drafted may provide 'good enough' information for the parties to consider a court-based or private FDR or indeed a civil/hybrid style mediation (lawyers present) where matters can hopefully be resolved without the necessity for a subsequent formal adjudication. Subject to the nature of the dispute, it may in some instances be appropriate to move immediately to some form of dispute resolution with only pleadings".

For the above reasons, it is not uncommon for a 'lighter' case management approach to the third-party claim to be adopted. Examples of such approach are listed in the Family Law Red Book which are as follows:

- Each party cases are pleaded, disclosure is ordered and then a FDR listed; or

- Each party is directed to plead their case and then the matter proceeds to a FDR; or

- Less commonly, the third party issue is heard during the final hearing; or

- In cases that are both factually and legally straightforward, directions are only made for the filing of witness statements with supporting documents exhibited. These documents are exchanged sequentially, and the matter proceeds to a FDR.

5.4. When should the preliminary issue hearing take place?

In financial remedy cases, there are three main hearings. The first is the First Appointment, followed by the Financial Dispute Resolution Appointment and if the parties are unable to reach an agreement, then they may need to be a final hearing. Where there is an intervenor claim, this issue is dealt with separately as standalone proceedings *usually* listed before the FDR appointment. Ideally, the preliminary issue hearing should not take place after the FDR or later than this as this can hold up the parties being able to negotiate and reach an agreement at the FDR. However, there is no fixed view of when a preliminary issue hearing should take place. From experience, depending on how factually complex or technical the preliminary issue may be, not having the preliminary hearing may limit the FDR judge's indication between the parties. There are other instances where parties can invite the judge to give an either-or indication, but there are most instances where some judges may not wish to proceed in this way as judges do not give indications on factual issues.

The timing of the preliminary issue hearing was briefly considered in *Shield v Shield* [2013] EWHC 3525 (Fam), which involved a marriage of no less than 43 years. In this case, there appeared to an intense conflict within the family in relation to certain dispositions which were, or may have been, made some years ago by the husband, and which may appear to have favoured the son in preference to the daughters and to be the disadvantage of the wife. The son was joined as an intervenor to the proceedings. The preliminary issue was identified as "whether the respondent's [viz the husband's] and/or the applicant's [viz the wife's] shareholdings in [the entire enterprise] are held on trust for the intervenor".[28] Upon the resolution of that issue hung potentially as much as £50m, or £25m, as it might have been accepted that, on any view, the son did own just over half the enterprise. Holman J was not willing to comment generally regarding the timing of an FDR, but he did observe that it would have been desirable and proportionate to have an FDR before the preliminary issue hearing given the facts of the case. Holman J observed:

> [17] But I do record my personal regret that in this particular case an FDR was not fixed before, rather than after, the trial of the preliminary issue. I am of course well aware of the argument and consideration that is invariably raised, that an FDR cannot be effective until it is known what the assets are. That may be a particularly cogent argument where there is a third party claim by somebody who is not himself part of the close family at all. In this particular case, the third party claim is made by a man who is the son of this husband and this wife. This entire litigation essentially concerns just three people: a mother, a father and their son, although I appreciate that it may impact also on the three daughters of the family. <u>I would have thought that in this case this was a particularly opportune moment to have assembled all concerned (not necessarily the husband himself if he was physically or mentally unfit to attend) in a forum such as an FDR and to have a sustained attempt to see if a resolution to this awful conflict could not be found at a stage when there may be high litigation risk for all concerned.</u>

28 *Shield v Shield* [2013] EWHC 3525 at [6].

Here, Holman J appeared to be indicating that when the third party is 'part of the close family' it may be more appropriate to have the individual attend court and explore the possibility of resolving the issue between the parties. This is also a useful approach to save costs. This can be contrasted with third-party individuals that are not particularly close to the parties.

At the preliminary issue hearing of *Shield v Shield* [2014] EWHC 23, Francis J stated:

> [**108**] I note that there was no FDR in relation to the preliminary issue. Whilst, as been made clear in a number of cases, an FDR will not necessarily be appropriate to the resolution of a preliminary issue, I express the view that consideration should at least be given to the possibility of an FDR prior to the hearing of a preliminary issue. It may well have been the case here that the input of an experienced FDR judge might have helped to save this family from the course which it has taken.

Applying the above, it is submitted that in a medium asset case where a further directions appointment might be disproportionate it may be sensible to reverse the order of the *TL v ML* directions, and invite the prospective intervenor to attend the FDR, on the basis that their application to be joined would be considered alongside the other directions if no agreement is reached.[29] Some arguments in favour of leaving the preliminary issue hearing until after the FDR can be that such approach avoids a further directions hearing and the costs of the same. This approach allows the prospective intervenor to become involved in the negotiations at court without the time and costs associated with undergoing the formal process where pleadings are

29 FPR r.9.17(9) makes it clear that after an unsuccessful FDR the court should make directions

required. Also, under this lighter approach priority is given to attempts to settle the whole case at the FDR before the parties are directed to comply with directions to file and serve pleadings, disclosure and witness statements, which can often be expensive.

Notwithstanding the benefits with this approach, arguments against leaving the preliminary issue hearing until after the FDR include the risk of the FDR becoming de-railed by the presence of an intervenor whose case has not been pleaded or set down in a witness statement. This can leave the FDR judge feeling unable to give an indication as to the merits of the preliminary issue. Equally, neither spouse will have had the opportunity to file evidence in response. This can pose practical difficulties during negotiations as the parties will be forced to conduct negotiations without knowing the strength of the other's case. Finally, given the nature of financial remedy proceedings, a prospective intervenor has no business seeing the Forms E, existing offers, or coming into court for a private hearing such as an FDR, save possibly in relation to the issue that concerns him.

5.5. Who has responsibility for joinder?

The question of who is responsible for joining a third party was considered in *Fisher Meredith v JH and PH (Financial Remedy: Appeal: Wasted Costs)* [2012] EWHC 408 (Fam) by Mostyn J. *Fisher* focused on two types of cases. The first concerned where a party asserts that the other party has an interest in an asset that is in the name of a third party. The second instance is where a party asserts that property to which they are legally entitled to is in fact beneficially owned by a third party. Mostyn J stated that in the first type of case, it is for the party asserting that the other party has an interest in an asset in the name of the third party that has responsibility to join the third party. In the second type of case, the obligation is on the party asserting that the property is beneficially owned by a third party or for that third party to apply for joinder.

5.6. Intervenor refuses to engage or join the proceedings

If a third party is not joined, that third party will not be bound by the court's decision. This is the position even when a third party has been given permission to intervene but has declined to do so and/or where they had knowledge of the proceedings and the issues at stake. An example of this problem occurred in *Richardson-Ruhan v Ruhan* [2017] EWHC 2739 (Fam) where findings were made that the third party was a nominee for the husband. The third party was invited to intervene but did not do so. As a result, the wife was later required to apply for the findings to apply to the third party. Overall, the importance of joinder was further confirmed in *Gourisaria v Gourisaria* in the Court of Appeal where Hughes LJ held that "a simple invitation to intervene is not by itself sufficient to produce an order which binds a third party who does not accept the invitation". Where a prospective intervenor does not answer the invitation, and issues no application to be joined, a third party can still be joined as a party on the application of a spouse or of the court's own motion.[30] It should be noted that the failure to join does not preclude the making of an assertion as to ownership at the enforcement stage.

5.7. Costs

There are two main costs regimes that apply in family proceedings. The general rule is that each party will be responsible for their own costs. These cost rules can be found in FPR 28.3, and this covers financial remedy proceedings. Under this rule, each party will pay

30 See para [18].

their own costs save for when applying the factors under the checklist in FPR 28.3(7):

> … In deciding what order (if any) to make under paragraph (6), the court must have regard to –
>
> (aa) any failure by a party, without good reason, to –
>
> (i) attend a MIAM (as defined in rule 3.1); or
>
> (ii) attend non-court dispute resolution;
>
> (a) any failure by a party to comply with these rules, any order of the court or any practice direction which the court considers relevant;
>
> (b) any open offer to settle made by a party;
>
> (c) whether it was reasonable for a party to raise, pursue or contest a particular allegation or issue;
>
> (d) the manner in which a party has pursued or responded to the application or a particular allegation or issue;
>
> (e) any other aspect of a party's conduct in relation to proceedings which the court considers relevant; and
>
> (f) the financial effect on the parties of any costs order.

The second cost regime that the court applies is the 'clean sheet' approach. In this regime, the court applies a broader discretion and may make 'such order as to costs as it thinks fit'.[31]

Intervenor claims often involve significant costs and delay. The outcomes in these cases are binary in that either the joined party succeeds in their case or fails to establish an interest in property. Costs application will naturally follow these cases. Intervenor claims are not governed by the general rule on costs, and instead, they are clean sheet cases, and therefore the stakes are high, particularly in modest to low asset cases (*Baker v Rowe* [2009] EWCA Civ 1162). At para 35 Ward LJ explained that:

> The orders might well have been made in ancillary relief proceedings, but they were not orders for nor even in connection with ancillary relief. The rule must be construed purposively as my Lord explained in Judge v Judge… and in his judgment above. Proceedings between intervenors do not come within the ambit of the rule. The judge making the costs order has, therefore, a wide discretion.

The extent to which the court will actually apply a wide discretion in considering what costs order should be made in an intervenor case is debatable. It is more likely that the clean sheet will be interpreted as involving a 'soft cost follow the event principle' (see *LM v DM (Costs Ruling)* [2021] EWFC 28). Thus, the stakes are high, particularly in modest to low asset cases. This highlights the high stakes of bringing or opposing intervenor claims. *Calderbank* offers are admissible. While the general rule at CPR 44.2 doesn't apply, success will normally be decisive on the 'clean sheet'.

31 Family Procedure Rules 2010, r 28.1.

As with intervenors that are individuals, parties seeking to join a third party should bear in mind that in the event that the third party succeeds in the preliminary issue between the parties, the third party can expect and indeed seek to recover their costs from the party who caused them to be joined. It follows that FPR 28.3 does not apply between the original party to the claim and the third party that intervenes. In light of this, parties wishing to join trustees to proceedings and who consequently fail to establish their case should be mindful of adverse cost consequences.

CHAPTER SIX

PRACTICAL TIPS RUNNING AND DEFENDING AN INTERVENOR CASE

6.1. Defending an Intervenor Claim

A classic intervenor example is as follows. The parties to a marriage become involved in financial remedy proceedings. Both parties complete their form E listing their assets including the properties that they own or hold an interest in. In completing his Form E, the husband lists one property and asserts that he holds that property on trust for the sole benefit of his elderly father. In support of this position, he refers discussions that took place between them at the time and money moving from the father to the husband towards the purchase. The father, eagerly supported by the husband, maintains that the money transferred from him towards the purchase speaks for itself and proves that the father has an interest in the property. Upon learning of the father's claim, the wife objects and asserts that she had always understood the property to be owned by the husband. However, she is unable to give direct evidence regarding the discussions relied upon by the husband and his father as she was never privy to them.

What defence could the wife raise to defend the intervenor claim raised by the husband's father above? For many parties in this position, the natural inclination is to argue that the claim is dodgy or simply untrue, which is insufficient in disputing such claims. As Munby J (as he then was) remarked in *A v A* [2007] 2 FLR 467 at [17]:

> "... a spouse who seeks to extend her claim for ancillary relief to assets which appear to be in the hands of someone other than her husband must identify, and by reference to established principle, some proper basis for doing so. The court cannot grant relief merely because the husband's arrangements appear to be artificial or even "dodgy".

Applying the above, it is submitted that the wife in this example, and others who find themselves defending intervenor claims, will have to advance an argument far stronger than the intervenor claim being 'dodgy' or untrue. This chapter therefore discusses how a party might defend an intervenor claim in such circumstances. The chapter considers the possible legal defences, the burden of proof, the importance of challenging documents as opposed to taking them purely at face value and the unreliability of oral evidence. At the end of the chapter, it should be understood that a party defending such claims has a number of weapons in their armoury. The chapter also gives an overview of how a prospective intervenor may want to advance their case in the event that they are joined to the proceedings.

6.1.1. The burden of proof: Who bears this?

The starting point in considering how best to defend an intervenor claim is to know who bears the burden of proof. It is well known that "the task of the judge determining a dispute as to ownership between a spouse and a third party is, of course, completely different in nature from the familiar discretionary exercise between spouses. A dispute with a third party must be approached on exactly the same legal basis as if it were being determined in the Chancery Division".[32] Consequently, directions should be given so that the parties can fully

32 *TL v ML and Others (Ancillary Relief: Claim Against Assets of Extended Family)* [2006] 1 FLR 1263 at [34].

plead their case, separate witness statements and a separate trial listed to determine the preliminary issue. In determining the preliminary issue, the hearing will be adversarial and not, 'quasi-inquisitorial' as is the case in financial remedies matters. The implications of this are that the trial judge will be concerned with determining whether the party upon whom the burden of proof lies has discharged it to the required degree of probability, rather than establishing the truth of what did or did not take place on a given occasion.

Given that it is the intervenor raising the existence of a beneficial interest or entitlement in property held by one of the spouses, the burden of proof lies on the party asserting the existence of a trust of land. This is typically the intervenor. In essence, it is for the intervenor to prove their cases on the balance of probabilities. If the intervenor fails to discharge the burden of proof, their intervention will naturally fail. There is no overarching duty on the court to consider the overall fairness of the outcome. Support for this position can be gleaned from the explanation given by Lord Hoffman in *Re B (Care Proceedings: Standard of Proof)* [2008] 2 FLR 141 at [2]:

> "... If a legal rule requires a fact to be proved (a "fact in issue), a judge or jury must decide whether or not it happened. There is no room for a finding that it might have happened. The law operates a binary system in which the only values are 0 and 1. The fact either happened or it did not. If the tribunal is left in doubt, the doubt is resolved by a rule that one party or the other carries the burden of proof. If the party who bears the burden of proof fails to discharge it, a value of 0 is returned and the fact is treated as not having happened. If he does discharge it, a value of 1 is returned and the fact is treated as having happened".

6.1.2. A legal defence

Aside from challenging the existence of a common intention constructive trust, proprietary estoppel or resulting trust, where there is a signed declaration of trust, consideration should be given to what defences can be advanced to challenge the document. Express declarations of trusts are determinative of beneficial ownership unless the declaration can be set aside for fraud, mistake or undue influence (*Pankhania v Chandegra* [2012] EWCA Civ 1438). In addition to this, a declaration can be challenged on the basis that it is a sham. The principles relating to 'sham' were comprehensively repeated in *ND v SD and Others* [2017] EWHC 1507 (Fam), where Roberts J concluded that:

> '[184] … two headline points emerge at the outset: (i) there must be a dishonest intent before the court will find an instrument to be a sham, and (ii) where instruments or agreements are properly and formally drawn (i.e. "perfectly proper agreements on their face"), absent a dishonest intent, there is a strong presumption that the parties intend to honour their rights and obligations thereunder
>
> …
>
> [186] … The next headline point… before transactions or documents will be construed by the court as sham transactions, all the parties to them must share a common intention that the documents themselves will not create the legal rights and obligations which they give the appearance of creating.'

thereunder.

6.1.3. Proper scrutinization of documents

Documentary evidence should be properly scrutinised and not taken at face value. The importance of this point was highlighted in the case of *Arif v Anwar and Rehan* [2015] EWHC 124 (Fam); [2016] 1 FLR 359, which concerned matrimonial proceedings where the court had to determine the beneficial ownership of the former matrimonial home as a preliminary issue. The husband's son from his first marriage contributed half of the estimated value of the property to pay for refurbishment works. He later claimed to have a 50% beneficial interest in the property in return. Norris J concluded that he could not place much reliance on the oral evidence or witness statements of the husband and intervenor. He stated that "...this is not a case in which I can treat the oral evidence as the primary source of reliable material. The recollection of each party is significantly coloured by what each sees as his or her best interests".[33] The trial judge considered the son's assertion that an agreement had been reached that he would receive a 50% beneficial interest in the property and explained the need for appropriate scrutiny. At paragraph 43 of the judgment, Norris J stated:

> '[43] ... The effect of any such agreement intended to have some legal effect is to make the registered title and the formal record of the beneficial ownerships materially inaccurate... so in my judgment such an agreement must be established on the balance of probabilities by clear evidence that has survived appropriate scrutiny. In most cases that scrutiny will arise from the fact that the existence of the constructive trust or the estoppel will be a matter of contention between parties to the alleged agreement or understanding, whose respective cases will be tested at trial. But that is not so in every case. Where the issue as to the existence of the agreement or understanding

33 See para 5.

> is not (in reality) being argued out between the parties to it then it is especially important to remember that the general policy of the law is that interests in land should be formally recorded and formally transferred and that policy would be defeated if interests in property could be readily transferred simply by conversations between the parties interested in a particular outcome which are not corroborated or otherwise soundly evidenced'.

The implications of the passage above is that where there is an intervenor and one party cannot give direct evidence in relation to the document, it is very important to remember the general policy of the law that interests in land are formally recorded, and any departure from that must be corroborated or 'soundly evidenced'.

6.1.4. Unreliability of Witness Oral Evidence: Re-evaluating the Court's Approach

> *"Above all, it is important to avoid the fallacy of supposing that, because a witness has confidence in his or her recollection and is honest, evidence based on that recollection provides any reliable guide to the truth"*

In these types of cases, it is very rare for the burden of proof to be discharged on oral evidence alone, without it being corroborated by contemporaneous documentary evidence. It follows that in defending an intervenor claim, the court should be invited to bear in mind the problems inherent in basing a decision on oral evidence, especially in relation to events that may have occurred long ago. This is due to it being acknowledged within the commercial courts that the human memory is fallible, and that it is difficult, if not impossible, to tell based on uncorroborated oral evidence if a witness is telling the truth.

In *Armagas Ltd v Mundogas SA* (*The Ocean Frost)* [1985] 1 Lloyds Rep 1, Robert Goff LJ commented at p.57:

> "...Speaking from my own experience, I have found it essential in cases of fraud, when considering the credibility of witnesses, always to test their veracity by reference to the objective facts proved independently of their testimony, in particular by reference to the documents in the case, and also to pay particular regard to their motives and to the overall probabilities. It is frequently very difficult to tell whether a witness is telling the truth or not; and where there is a conflict of evidence such as there was in the present case, reference to the objective facts and documents, references to the witness' motives and to the overall probabilities can be of very great assistance to a Judge in ascertaining the truth."

The fallibility of the human memory was addressed in the High Court commercial case of *Gestmin SGPS SA v Credit Suisse (UK) Ltd* [2013] EWHC 3560 (Comm). In *Gestmin*, Mr Justice Leggatt was tasked with evaluating the evidence of a number of witnesses concerning various events that took place over a number of years. In his judgment, Leggatt J devoted several passages where he considered the psychology of recollection, psychological research and what we currently know about the fallibility of human memory of events. Key passages are as follows:

> [17] ... Psychological research has demonstrated that memories are fluid and malleable, being constantly rewritten whenever they are retrieved... External information can intrude into a witness's memory, as can his or her own thoughts and beliefs, and both can cause dramatic changes in recollection. Events can come to be recalled as memories which did not happen at all or which happened to someone

else (referred to in the literature as a failure of source memory).

Moreover, the process of civil litigation itself can subject the memories of witnesses to powerful biases, as naturally, the nature of litigation is such that witnesses generally have a stake in a particular version of facts being established.[34] For example, in an intervenor case, the intervenor has an interest in establishing their case and persuading the court that they hold the interest that they do within property. The human memory can also be interfered with considerably in civil litigation through preparing for trial, including the drafting of witness statements:

> [20] … A witness is asked to make a statement, often (as in the present case) when a long time has already elapsed since the relevant events. The statement is usually drafted for the witness by a lawyer who is inevitably conscious of the significance for the issues in the case of what the witness does nor does not say. The statement is made after the witness's memory has been "refreshed" by reading documents. The documents considered often include statements of case and other argumentative material as well as documents which the witness did not see at the time or which came into existence after the events which he or she is being asked to recall. The statement may go through several iterations before it is finalised. Then, usually months later, the witness will be asked to re-read his or her statement and review documents again before giving evidence in court. The effect of this process is to establish in the mind of the witness the matters recorded in his or her own statement and other written material, whether they be true or false, and to cause the witness's memory of events to be based increasingly on this material and later

34 *Gestmin*, see para [19].

> interpretations of it rather than on the original experience of the events.
>
> ...
>
> [22] In the light of these considerations, the best approach for a judge to adopt in the trial of a commercial case is, in my view, to place little if any reliance at all on witnesses' recollections of what was said in meetings and conversations, and to base factual findings on inferences drawn from the documentary evidence and known or probable facts. This does not mean that oral testimony serves no useful purpose – though its utility is often disproportionate to its length... Above all, it is important to avoid the fallacy of supposing that, because a witness has confidence in his or her recollection and is honest, evidence based on that recollection provides any reliable guide to the truth.

Overall, the key points to be distilled from these passages are as follows:

- The memories of witnesses can be subjected to powerful biases as a result of the process of civil litigation. This can include the drafting of witness statements.

- The effect of drafting the witness statement and referring to documents establishes in the mind of the witness the matters documented in their own statement and other written material. This is the case whether they are true or false, and the effect is to cause the witness's memory of events to be based increasingly on this material instead of their original experience of the events.

- The mere fact that a witness is confident in their recollection does not mean that their recollection will be accurate, and as Leggatt J noted, this is particularly true when recalling past beliefs.

Finally, whilst this was a commercial case, Mostyn J reviewed *Gestmin* in *Lachaux v Lachaux* [2017] EWHC 385, a family law case involving a jurisdictional dispute with the United Arab Emirates. In *Lachaux*, Mostyn J concluded that the guidance in *Gestmin* had wider application and were not confined to cases of commercial fraud. He observed that:

> [37] ... These wise words are surely of general application and are not confined to fraud cases (although this case includes allegations of fraud). It is certainly often difficult to tell whether a witness is telling the truth, and I agree with the view of Mr Justice Bingham that the demeanour of a witness is not a reliable pointer to his or her honesty'.

Since then, the principles set out in *Gestmin* have been applied and considered in a number of cases and the need to approach witness recollection with caution is borne in the mind of judges when determining matters. For example, in *Sadie Briggs (Widow and Administratrix of the Estate of Brian Briggs) v Drylined Homes Limited*, a claim for damages arising from the deceased contracting and dying from an asbestos-related cancer. In determining the matter, Dexter Dias KC sitting as a Deputy High Court Judge (as he then was) outlined what he called the Thirteen Axioms of Fact-Finding. Of the thirteen axioms of fact-finding that he drew together, some included:

> (8) There are important and recognised limits on the reliability of human memory: (a) our memory is a notoriously imperfect and fallible recording device; (b) a greater confidence displayed by a witness does not necessarily

correlate with a correspondingly more accurate recollection; (c) the process of civil litigation subjects the memory to "powerful biases", particularly where a witness has a "tie of loyalty" to a party (*Gestmin SCPS S.A. v Credit Suisse (UK) Ltd* EWHC 3560 (Comm) at [15]-[22], per Leggatt J (as then was)).

…

(10) Contemporary documents are 'always of the utmost importance' (*Onassis v Vergottis* [1968] 2 Lloyd's Rep. 403 at 431, per Lord Pearce), but in their absence, greater weight will be placed on inherent probability or improbability of witness's accounts: "It is necessary to bear in mind, however, that this is not one of those cases in which the accounts given by the witnesses can be tested by reference to a body of contemporaneous documents. As a result, the judge was forced to rely heavily on his assessment of the witnesses and the inherent plausibility or implausibility of their accounts". (*Jafari-Fini v Skillglass* Ltd [2007] EWCA Civ 261 at [80], per Moore-Bick LJ);

"Faced with documentary lacunae of this nature, the judge has little choice but to fall back on considerations such as the overall plausibility of the evidence" (*NatWest Markets Plc v Bilta (UK) Ltd* [2021] EWCA Civ 680 at [50], per Asplin, Andrews and Birss LJJ, jointly.

Running an Intervenor Claim

6.1.5. Clear instructions and understand the position

Skilful client interviewing skills are essential to identifying the issues in the case clearly and early. Within the first or second client conference, the assets of the marriage and how they are held should be clearly understood. The starting point is to understand in whose name the property was purchased. The purpose for the purchase is also relevant including why the property was purchased in the way it was.

The following questions and information should also be ascertained by the lawyer:

1) Whose name is on the title register for the property?

    a. Obtain an official copy entry from the Land Registry

    b. Acquire the transfer document ("TR1"). As will be seen below, this document is very important, depending on which side of the case you are on. If you are the intervenor, you will be looking at whether the transfer document contains an express declaration of trust.

2) Did any third party contribute to the purchase of the property? If so, how much? Where did the funds come from?

3) Did any third parties provide loans/gifts to the parties during the marriage which may be argued or perceived as granting the third party a beneficial interest in the property?

4) Did the parties own one or more commercial or buy-to-let properties with business partners. If so, whether they have formally identified their respective interests in the properties.

5) Is there any documentary evidence of discussions between the parties in respect of their interests in the property. Such documentary evidence can include text messages, emails, cohabitation agreements, love letters etc.

If any of these enquiries leads to the conclusion that the third party may have an interest in the property or may lead to their potential involvement, then this should be borne in mind and the joinder process considered as early as possible. This can include raising this in correspondence with the other side, identifying the existence of such issue in the party's Form E etc. It does not mean, however, that the entire joinder process should be embarked upon fully. The merits of any third party issues should always be assessed due to the risk of cost consequences if the case is poor. It is also important to bear in mind the principle of proportionality and consider alternative ways to resolve the issue before embarking on the formal *TL v ML* procedure.

6.1.6. Obtain the conveyancing file

After taking instructions, the next step is to obtain the conveyancing file and to look at what is in it. The intervenor should be looking for any documentation that supports their claim and also any documents that undermine their case. The first document to be sought is the Transfer Deed. Those documents can provide express declarations of trust, and they are binding absent fraud, duress or mistake. If the declaration of trust was prepared separately from the transfer deed, this document should be obtained and any discussions recorded leading up to this. This can make or break the case particularly as the intervenor must plead their case and there can be costs implications if the case is hopeless. Intervenors or their legal representatives should also check if there are any attendance notes on the file or letters of advice given concerning ownership of the property and the parties' beneficial shares.

The correspondence should be looked at. Some of the questions that need answering include why the property was purchased in the sole name of one party when funds came from both parties or a third party; why was purchased in joint names at all; and why, if the property was purchased in joint names without declaration of trust, did one party put more money down than the other? The final step is to obtain bank statements if they are still available from the time of purchase. These should be scrutinised and to see if they are consistent with what the intervenor says about the purchase or their interest in the property. Obtaining bank statements help establish who paid for what and the timing of this, as they can be useful in understanding the parties' intentions.

6.1.7. One form of evidence should not be inappropriately elevated over another

The recollection of witnesses and the fallibility of the human memory, with reference to observations made by Leggatt J (as he then was) in *Gestmin* was discussed in the section above. On the one hand, in defending an intervenor claim, one may argue that the court's enquiry should be based primarily on contemporaneous documentary evidence. However, later authorities suggest that a more balanced approach should be adopted, which can be a useful rebuttal point to parties that wish to invite the court to elevate one form of evidence over another. In essence, whilst there is recognition of the fact that oral evidence of witnesses is often critical, it should be recognised that it has its limitations. Support for this can be found in *Re A (A Child)* [2020] EWCA Civ 1230, which concerned an appeal against an order at the conclusion of a fact-finding hearing within private child law proceedings. In *Re A*, King LJ considered legal guidance in relation to issues of credibility, demeanour and memory in the context of a fact-finding process in private child law proceedings, and legal guidance from family and wider jurisdictions.

In considering guidance from other cases, King LJ referred to the case of *Kogan v Martin and Others* [2019] EWCA Civ 1645, where the judge embarked on a lengthy consideration of the reliability, as a general matter, of the recollection of witnesses. In *Kogan* at first instance, the judge had wrongly regarded Leggatt J's statements in *Gestmin* and *Blue v Ashley* [2017] EWHC 1928 (Comm) as an "admonition" against placing any reliance at all on the recollection of witnesses "of what was said in meetings and conversations and instead base factual findings on inferences drawn from documentary evidence and known or probable facts".[35] Per para 88 in *Kogan*, the Court of Appeal said:

> "We start by recalling that the judge read Leggatt J's statements in *Gestmin v Credit Suisse* and *Blue v Ashley* as an "admonition" against placing any reliance at all on the recollections of witnesses. We consider that to have been a serious error in the present case for a number of reasons. First, as has very recently been noted by HHJ Gore QC in *CBX v North West Anglia NHS Trust* [2019] 7 WLUK 57, *Gestmin* is not to be taken as laying down any general principle for the assessment of evidence. It is one of a line of distinguished judicial observations that emphasise the fallibility of human memory and the need to assess witness evidence in its proper place alongside contemporaneous documentary evidence and evidence upon which undoubted or probable reliance can be placed. Earlier statements of this kind are discussed by Lord Bingham in his well-known essay *The Judge as Juror: The Judicial Determination of Factual Issues* (from The Business of Judging, Oxford 2000). But a proper awareness of the fallibility of memory does not relieve judges of the task of making findings of fact based upon all of the evidence.

35 *Kogan*, see para 70.

> Heuristics or mental short cuts are no substitute for this essential judicial function. In particular, where a party's sworn evidence is disbelieved, the court must say why that is; it cannot simply ignore the evidence".

It is for this reason, inter alia, that the Court of Appeal in *Kogan* "emphasised the need for a balanced approach to the significance of oral evidence regardless of jurisdiction".[36] Referring to the judgment, King LJ in *Re A* noted that whilst *Kogan* concerned a copyright dispute between former partners, the judgment was a judgment of the court with wider implications. It follows that in intervenor cases, the third party may argue that whilst oral evidence has its limitations, the court should nonetheless take a balanced approach to all the evidence, and if oral testimony is not going to be accepted, it should clearly explain why and not be ignored in preference for documentary evidence. Moreover, *Gestmin* should not be taken as laying down a general principle for the assessment of evidence. Rather, the court's function remains to make findings of fact based on all the evidence available to it, and awareness of the fallibility of the human memory does not relieve judges of that role. As concluded by King LJ in *Re A* at [41]:

> [41] The court must, however, be mindful of the fallibility of memory and the pressures of giving evidence. The relative significance of oral and contemporaneous evidence will vary from case to case. What is important, as was highlighted in Kogan, is that the court assesses all the evidence in a manner suited to the case before it and does not inappropriately elevate one kind of evidence over another.

36 *Re A (A Child)*, see para [**36**].

CONCLUSION

The purpose of this book was to explore the role of third-party interests in financial remedy proceedings and provide practical guidance on how to approach these cases when they arise in our practice, either as lawyers, or litigants in person. In financial remedy proceedings, the court may only make orders in respect of the property owned by the parties to the marriage, and not that belonging to third parties. The book has shown that where a party outside those to the marriage, known as a third party, claims to have an interest in property which is held solely or jointly by the parties to the marriage, it will be necessary for the court to determine the extent of the third parties interest in the property and how that interest should be dealt with within the proceedings. Such third-party interest could be a family member who has advanced capital towards the purchase of the family home or another property which is held by one or both parties to the marriage, or even trustees.

Where the potential for a third-party interest arises in proceedings, this should be identified and made known to the court and the other side as soon as reasonably practicable. This can be when Form Es are exchanged and certainly at the First Appointment so appropriate directions can be made to deal with the matter. The court may also take steps to serve the third party with notice of the proceedings so that they can become involved in a cost effective and timely manner. Ultimately, where a third party asserts that they hold an interest in property which is subject to the proceedings, the third party may be joined to the proceedings as an intervenor in order to determine that issue. This is formerly known as joinder. Pursuant to rule 9.26B of the Family Procedure Rules 2010 ("FPR 2010"), "the court may direct that a person or body be added as a party to proceedings for a financial remedy if it is desirable to add the new party so that the court can resolve all the matters in dispute in the proceedings" or it is desirable to a new party so that the court can resolve an issue involving the new party and an existing party which is connected to the matters in dispute in the proceedings. In essence, the joining of the third party must be desirable.

Whilst the test of joinder is one of desirability, it should not be forgotten that joining an intervenor is a step which has significant consequences in terms of the duration and cost of the proceedings. Apart from desirability, it should be firmly borne in mind whether the joining of the third party is proportionate. This is because in some cases, the introduction of a third party and the requirement for pleadings etc. can lead to excessive costs, such that the exercise becomes disproportionate to the overall assets in the matrimonial pot. Further, where joinder will generally be desirable where an issue arises as to the ownership of real property, it may not be desirable, or even proportionate, where the issue is an alleged loan.

Although r. 9.26B, sets out the rules to joining a party to proceedings, in practice, many courts do not follow it. Rather, courts can invite a party to write to the court stating if they wish to intervene, at which stage they are granted party status. This is not what r 9.26B (5) requires, as the rules state that there **"must"** be a Part 18 application, supported by evidence (save, obviously, where an intervenor is joined of the court's own motion). Where an intervenor refuses to engage, the obligation to seek his joinder falls not upon the applicant but the party who relies on / supports the intervenor's claim. The question of joining a trustee is a complicated one, where (in terms of an application to vary a nuptial settlement) there is a conflict in the authorities. In terms of directions and procedural case management, the seminal authority of *TL v ML* remains.

The fundamental point to bear in mind in every intervention involving property claims is that the dispute is to be determined by the application of principles (generally) of trust law and property law, and not the exercise of a broad-based discretion. Where an intervenor dispute is asymmetrical (i.e. the wife cannot give direct evidence on the husband or intervenor's case) the court should nevertheless consider the burden of proof, the inherent difficulties in oral recollection, apply 'proper scrutiny' to documentary evidence and (in some cases) consider whether a declaration of trust was intended to be effective. Finally, costs will generally be at large as intervenor cases fall outside the scope of FPR 2010, r. 28.3.

MORE BOOKS BY LAW BRIEF PUBLISHING

A selection of our other titles available now:-

'A Practical Guide to Probation Breaches and Other Applications' by Mark Thomas
'A Practical Guide to Remarriage and Divorce' by Cordelia Williams & Claire Howard
'A Practical Guide to Privacy, Transparency, Reporting Restrictions and Closed Proceedings in the Court of Protection' by Laura Mannering
'Beaumont on Barristers – A Guide to Defending Disciplinary Proceedings (Second Edition)' by Marc Beaumont
'A Practical Guide to Payments for Environmental Services' by Ben Sharples
'A Practical Guide to the Law of Pregnancy and Maternity at Work' by Rebecca Thomas
'A Practical Guide to Redundancy – Second Edition' by Philip Hyland & Collette Moore
'A Practical Guide to International Issues for Scottish Family Lawyers' by Susie Mountain, Donna McKay, Ken MacDonald
'A Practical Guide to the Law on Deprivation of Liberty' by Ben Troke
'A Practical Guide to Rights over Airspace and Subsoil – Second Edition' by Daniel Gatty
'A Practical Guide to the Law in Relation to Inquests' by Ramya Nagesh
'A Practical Guide to the Construction and Rectification of Wills and Trust Instruments (Second Edition)' by Edward Hewitt
'A Practical Guide to Data Protection in Social Housing' by Clare Paterson
'A Practical Guide to Spousal Maintenance – Second Edition' by Liz Cowell
'A Practical Guide to International Parental Child Abduction Law (England and Wales)' by Dr Onyója Momoh
'A Practical Guide to Deprivation of British Citizenship' by Sean Ell
'A Practical Guide to Commercial Property Service Charges' by Rachel Garton
'A Practical Guide to Clinical Negligence – Third Edition' by Geoffrey Simpson-Scott (Geoff)
'A Practical Guide to the Rights of Grandparents in Children Proceedings – Second Edition' by Stuart Barlow

'The Electronic Communications Code: A Practical Guide – Second Edition' by Kerry Bretherton KC, James Castle, Mark Loveday
'A Practical Guide to the Independent School Standards – September 2023 Edition' by Sarah McKimm
'A Practical Guide to Estate Administration and Crypto Assets' by Richard Marshall
'A Practical Guide to Parental Alienation in Private and Public Law Children Cases' by Sam King QC & Frankie Shama
'Contested Heritage – Removing Art from Land and Historic Buildings' by Richard Harwood QC, Catherine Dobson, David Sawtell
'The Limits of Separate Legal Personality: When Those Running a Company Can Be Held Personally Liable for Losses Caused to Third Parties Outside of the Company' by Dr Mike Wilkinson
'A Practical Guide to Transgender Law' by Robin Moira White & Nicola Newbegin
'A Practical Guide to 'Stranded Spouses' in Family Law' by Mani Singh Basi
'A Practical Guide to Residential Freehold Conveyancing' by Lorraine Richardson
'A Practical Guide to Pensions on Divorce for Lawyers' by Bryan Scant
'A Practical Guide to Challenging Sham Marriage Allegations in Immigration Law' by Priya Solanki
'A Practical Guide to Digital Communications Evidence in Criminal Law' by Sam Willis
'A Practical Guide to Legal Rights in Scotland' by Sarah-Jane Macdonald
'A Practical Guide to New Build Conveyancing' by Paul Sams & Rebecca East
'A Practical Guide to Inherited Wealth on Divorce' by Hayley Trim
'A Practical Guide to Practice Direction 12J and Domestic Abuse in Private Law Children Proceedings' by Rebecca Cross & Malvika Jaganmohan
'A Practical Guide to Confiscation and Restraint' by Narita Bahra QC, John Carl Townsend, David Winch
'A Practical Guide to the Law of Forests in Scotland' by Philip Buchan
'A Practical Guide to Health and Medical Cases in Immigration Law' by Rebecca Chapman & Miranda Butler
'A Practical Guide to Bad Character Evidence for Criminal Practitioners by Aparna Rao
'A Practical Guide to Extradition Law post-Brexit' by Myles Grandison et al
'A Practical Guide to Hoarding and Mental Health for Housing Lawyers' by Rachel Coyle

'Stephens on Contractual Indemnities' by Richard Stephens
'A Practical Guide to the EU Succession Regulation' by Richard Frimston
'A Practical Guide to Solicitor and Client Costs – Second Edition' by Robin Dunne
'Constructive Dismissal – Practice Pointers and Principles' by Benjimin Burgher
'A Practical Guide to Religion and Belief Discrimination Claims in the Workplace' by Kashif Ali
'A Practical Guide to the Law of Medical Treatment Decisions' by Ben Troke
'Fundamental Dishonesty and QOCS in Personal Injury Proceedings: Law and Practice' by Jake Rowley
'A Practical Guide to the Law in Relation to School Exclusions' by Charlotte Hadfield & Alice de Coverley
'A Practical Guide to Divorce for the Silver Separators' by Karin Walker
'The Right to be Forgotten – The Law and Practical Issues' by Melissa Stock
'A Practical Guide to Planning Law and Rights of Way in National Parks, the Broads and AONBs' by James Maurici QC, James Neill et al
'A Practical Guide to Election Law' by Tom Tabori
'A Practical Guide to the Law in Relation to Surrogacy' by Andrew Powell
'A Practical Guide to Claims Arising from Fatal Accidents – Second Edition' by James Patience
'A Practical Guide to Asbestos Claims' by Jonathan Owen & Gareth McAloon
'A Practical Guide to Stamp Duty Land Tax in England and Northern Ireland' by Suzanne O'Hara
'A Practical Guide to the Law of Farming Partnerships' by Philip Whitcomb
'A Practical Guide to the Law of Unlawful Eviction and Harassment – Second Edition' by Stephanie Lovegrove
'A Practical Guide to Costs in Personal Injury Claims – Second Edition' by Matthew Hoe
'A Practical Guide to the General Data Protection Regulation (GDPR) – Second Edition' by Keith Markham
'A Practical Guide to Working with Litigants in Person and McKenzie Friends in Family Cases' by Stuart Barlow
'Protecting Unregistered Brands: A Practical Guide to the Law of Passing Off' by Lorna Brazell
'A Practical Guide to Secondary Liability and Joint Enterprise Post-Jogee' by Joanne Cecil & James Mehigan

'A Practical Guide to the Pre-Action RTA Claims Protocol for Personal Injury Lawyers' by Antonia Ford

'A Practical Guide to Neighbour Disputes and the Law' by Alexander Walsh

'A Practical Guide to Coercive Control for Legal Practitioners and Victims' by Rachel Horman

'A Practical Guide to the Law of Driverless Cars – Second Edition'

by Alex Glassbrook, Emma Northey & Scarlett Milligan

'A Practical Guide to TOLATA Claims' by Greg Williams

'A Practical Guide to Elderly Law – Second Edition' by Justin Patten

'A Practical Guide to Responding to Housing Disrepair and Unfitness Claims' by Iain Wightwick

'A Practical Guide to the Law of Bullying and Harassment in the Workplace' by Philip Hyland

'How to Be a Freelance Solicitor: A Practical Guide to the SRA-Regulated Freelance Solicitor Model' by Paul Bennett

'A Practical Guide to Prison Injury Claims' by Malcolm Johnson

'A Practical Guide to Advising Clients at the Police Station' by Colin Stephen McKeown-Beaumont

'A Practical Guide to Antisocial Behaviour Injunctions – Second Edition' by Iain Wightwick

'Practical Mediation: A Guide for Mediators, Advocates, Advisers, Lawyers, and Students in Civil, Commercial, Business, Property, Workplace, and Employment Cases' by Jonathan Dingle with John Sephton

'The Mini-Pupillage Workbook' by David Boyle

'A Practical Guide to Crofting Law' by Brian Inkster

'A Practical Guide to the Law of Domain Names and Cybersquatting' by Andrew Clemson

'A Practical Guide to the Law of Gender Pay Gap Reporting' by Harini Iyengar

'NHS Whistleblowing and the Law' by Joseph England

'Employment Law and the Gig Economy' by Nigel Mackay & Annie Powell

'A Practical Guide to Noise Induced Hearing Loss (NIHL) Claims' by Andrew Mckie, Ian Skeate, Gareth McAloon

'An Introduction to Beauty Negligence Claims – A Practical Guide for the Personal Injury Practitioner' by Greg Almond

'Intercompany Agreements for Transfer Pricing Compliance' by Paul Sutton

'Zen and the Art of Mediation' by Martin Plowman

'A Practical Guide to Adoption for Family Lawyers' by Graham Pegg

'A Practical Guide to Industrial Disease Claims' by Andrew Mckie & Ian Skeate
'A Practical Guide to Conducting a Sheriff Court Proof' by Andrew Stevenson
'A Practical Guide to Vicarious Liability' by Mariel Irvine
'A Practical Guide to Applications for Landlord's Consent and Variation of Leases' by Mark Shelton
'A Practical Guide to Relief from Sanctions Post-Mitchell and Denton' by Peter Causton
'A Practical Guide to Equity Release for Advisors' by Paul Sams
'A Practical Guide to Financial Services Claims' by Chris Hegarty
'A Practical Guide to Financial Ombudsman Service Claims' by Adam Temple & Robert Scrivenor
'A Practical Guide to Running Housing Disrepair and Cavity Wall Claims – Second Edition' by Andrew Mckie & Ian Skeate
'A Practical Guide to Holiday Sickness Claims – Second Edition' by Andrew Mckie & Ian Skeate
'Arguments and Tactics for Personal Injury and Clinical Negligence Claims' by Dorian Williams
'A Practical Guide to Drone Law' by Rufus Ballaster, Andrew Firman, Eleanor Clot
'On Experts: CPR35 for Lawyers and Experts' by David Boyle
'An Introduction to Personal Injury Law' by David Boyle

These books and more are available to order online direct from the publisher at www.lawbriefpublishing.com, where you can also read free sample chapters. For any queries, call us on 0844 587 2383 or email us at mail@lawbriefpublishing.com.

Our books are all generally in stock at www.amazon.co.uk with free next day delivery for Prime members, and at good legal bookshops such as Wildy & Sons.

We are regularly launching new books in our series of practical day-to-day practitioners' guides. Visit our website and join our free newsletter to be kept informed and to receive special offers, free chapters, etc.

You can also follow us on Twitter at www.twitter.com/lawbriefpub.

www.ingramcontent.com/pod-product-compliance
Lightning Source LLC
LaVergne TN
LVHW022304200926
848481LV00004B/1214

* 9 7 8 1 9 1 4 6 0 8 9 7 1 *